The Kindness Curriculum

Other Redleaf books by Judith Anne Rice

Those Itsy-Bitsy Teeny-Tiny Not So Nice Head Lice

Those Icky Sticky Smelly Cavity-Causing but . . . Invisible Germs

Those Mean Nasty Dirty Downright Disgusting but . . . Invisible Germs

Those Ooey Gooey Winky Blinky but . . . Invisible Pinkeye Germs

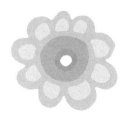

Second Edition

The Kindness
Curriculum

STOP BULLYING BEFORE IT STARTS

Judith Anne Rice

Redleaf Press®
www.redleafpress.org
800-423-8309

Published by Redleaf Press
10 Yorkton Court
St. Paul, MN 55117
www.redleafpress.org

First edition published 1995. Second edition 2013.
Cover design by Jim Handrigan
Cover photograph by Veer/Diego Cervo
Interior design by Erin Kirk New
Typeset in Berkeley Oldstyle Medium and Franklin Gothic Book
Illustrations by Becky Radtke
Printed in the United States of America
20 19 18 17 16 15 14 13   1 2 3 4 5 6 7 8

Library of Congress Cataloging-in-Publication Data
Rice, Judith, 1953–
    The kindness curriculum : stop bullying before it starts / Judith Anne Rice.—Second Edition.
        pages cm
    Summary: "Use this comprehensive framework and developmentally appropriate activities to teach
young children compassion, conflict resolution, respect, and other positive, pro-social values as you
cultivate a peaceful and supportive learning environment for all children." —Provided by publisher.
    Includes bibliographical references.
    ISBN 978-1-60554-124-2 (pbk.)
    ISBN 978-1-60554-256-0 (e-book)
    1. Moral education (Early childhood) 2. Social values—Study and teaching (Early childhood)
3. Early childhood education—Activity programs.   I. Title.
    LB1139.35.M67R53 2013
    370.11'4—dc23
                                2012039886

Printed on acid-free paper

In memory of Colin Jay Petersen, a loving child

August 23, 1985 to September 29, 1999

Kindness is the golden chain by which society is bound together.

—Goethe

Contents

Acknowledgments

I am grateful to Redleaf Press and especially to Jan Zita Grover.

To the Eller girls, Lorraine and Elaine, I am continuously thankful for my most cherished life lessons. They don't make them like you two anymore.

 # Introduction

Parents want their children to be happy. Can we teach happy? Yes, because happiness comes from compassion for others and contentment within ourselves, and those values are what the activities in this book help develop.

This book is intended for family child care settings, child care centers, the home, Head Start programs, preschools, hospitals, homeless shelters, and anywhere young children are being cared for.

Young children learn from the repetition of concrete experience. The fun activities in this book help them develop compassion for others by practicing simple, powerful lessons that incrementally foster love, feelings and empathy, gentleness, self-control, respect, friendship, and conflict resolution.

Organization of the Book

Each of the first eight chapters of *The Kindness Curriculum* involves a building block of character development. These chapters contain activities that are new or revised since the first edition.

The first chapter, "Creating Calm," sets the stage for prosocial play. Calm children are better able to choose positive behavior than are stressed-out ones, who may feel out of control. Activities in this chapter help children feel calm and choose kindness. The next four chapters deal with the fundamental values of love, feelings and empathy, gentleness, and respect. In these chapters, children are introduced to the concepts of unselfishness, understanding, and valuing themselves and others. The following three chapters, "Self-Control," "Friendship," and "Conflict Resolution," provide experience in dealing with others in constructive and enriching ways.

Chapter 8, "Conflict Resolution," is designed to help prevent bullying before it starts. The goal here is to cut off potential bullying behaviors before they become entrenched and to build up resilience/resistance to hurtful behavior. With consistent and systematic repetition of the problem-solving activities in this chapter, you are likely to see a strong impact on the level of cooperation among the children. As a result, your learning environment will function more smoothly.

In chapter 9, children learn about the powerful technique of visualization, an effective tool for improving behavior, boosting learning skills, and fostering creativity.

The activities in each chapter are fun and easy to implement. You will find that children love them for the expression they allow and the playfulness they provide. As a group, the activities create an atmosphere of acceptance, empowerment, and love, encouraging children to seek out the goodness in themselves and each other. Many of the activities have their strongest impact when incorporated into daily routines instead of being used in a unit approach. For example, The Kindness Pledge, found in chapter 2, can be recited at the beginning of each day.

Because parents are the most powerful force in children's lives, it is important to encourage their participation in their children's education. For this reason, I have included chapter 10, "Parent and Child Home Sweet Homework." Photocopy the exercises, and send them home with the children to be completed and returned.

At the end of the book are two useful appendixes and lists of recommended resources. The first appendix is filled with reproducible forms to be used with some of the activities. (These forms also can be downloaded from www.redleafpress.org.) The second provides a number of common American Sign Language (ASL) signs that provide visual behavioral cues for children. The lists of recommended resources include children's books, books for teachers, and websites that enhance the curriculum.

A Few Words about Bullying

In the years since the first edition of *The Kindness Curriculum*, bullying has gained prominence as a problem that the educational system must address. This new edition addresses bullying, with this qualification: I think it is unfair to think of preschoolers as bullies. At this age, children are experimenting with behaviors and must be guided in appropriate ways to deal with their emotions.

Preschool provides a window of opportunity for preventing or reducing the severity of later bullying behavior. Because the brains of young children are developing and their habits are forming in response to social interactions, modeling, and the environment, it is crucial that young children be exposed to loving values, which constitute the building blocks for positive character development. Activities that reinforce positive behavior can serve as preemptive strikes against bullying. It is the responsibility of adults to set clear and simple limits and then observe and work together with children when bullying behavior begins to surface.

Successful adult supervision must also include limiting children's exposure to violent media. The American Psychological Association declares that "viewing mass media violence leads to increases in aggressive attitudes, values, and behavior, particularly in children, and has a long-lasting effect on behavior and personality, including criminal behavior." So, if the values promoted in this book are to prevail, we must not let them be overwhelmed by the powerful influences of popular culture.

Chapter 1   Creating Calm

Calmness is the cradle of power.
—J. G. Holland

Calm children are better able to choose positive behavior than stressed-out ones, who may feel out of control. This chapter contains activities that help children be calm and choose kindness.

Practicing deep breathing is a quick way to calm down children's nervous systems, lower their heart rates, lower the blood pressure of their busy bodies, and boost their immune systems. If children practice deep breathing regularly, you will notice a difference in their behavior. When I first introduced one of my classes to breathing awareness and simple yoga poses, the initial results were chaotic. But over time, the children really looked forward to the exercises, took pride in their abilities, and demonstrated a lot of cooperation. Deep breathing will also help you relax, recharge, and enjoy.

I have called activity 12 "Freshersize," which is a playful word I made up to describe activities that blend fresh air with exercise—in other words, playing outdoors. Children today spend more time indoors than ever before, and doing so comes at a cost to their mental, physical, and spiritual health. Children are no longer herded outside to play freely. More and more children experience life and social interactions virtually, through computers, text messages, e-mail, video games, and television. Freshersize activities describe ways to reconnect children with nature.

I also encourage you to teach some simple yoga poses, because they will help you de-stress along with the children. Yoga differs from traditional exercises by recognizing the importance of the mind-body connection. It's more effective for improving not just physical but also mental and emotional health.

1

Practicing Quiet

Purpose

To help children experience quiet

Materials   A variety of pictures of quiet and loud objects

Procedure   Many children live in busy households where being loud is the norm. Even children who live in calm households need to learn that it's good to be quiet sometimes. Knowing how to be quiet helps children listen, learn, and show respect. Here are some ways to engage children in identifying and engaging in quiet behavior:

- Gather objects and pictures of objects that are either quiet or loud. Prepare two trays, each labeled with an image of a quiet or loud object and the words *Quiet* or *Loud*. Ask the children to sort the objects and pictures onto the appropriate tray. Or place the objects in a bag, pull them out one at a time, and ask the children to identify each one as loud or quiet.

- Here are some examples of quiet and loud objects:

Quiet	Loud
feathers	whistle
bubbles	drums
stuffed toys	honking horn
cotton balls	cymbals
scarves	picture of a train
picture of a mouse	picture of a motorcycle
picture of a rabbit	picture of a garbage truck
picture of a rainbow	picture of lightning

- Help the children identify differences between sounds by playing commercial listening games or by creating your own quiet and loud sounds on an audio recording.

- Ask the children to quietly search for quiet things around the room.

- To reduce stress, make quiet time a part of every day.

Read   *Quiet Loud* by Leslie Patricelli (2003)

2

Sweet Spots

Purpose

To provide "sweet spots" in the room—areas that can serve as children's personal spaces, where they can enjoy a sense of privacy and peacefulness that is hard to come by in a room filled with other children

Materials   Various

Procedure   Use these ideas to create sweet spots in your room:

- Ask the children to paint and decorate a large, empty appliance box. Fill it with pillows. Make a skylight by cutting a hole in the top, or provide a flashlight. Leave one side open so you can observe what is going on inside.

- Provide an egg-shaped chair called the PS Lömsk swivel chair, which Ikea sells. The child can pull down the polyester hood and block out the world. Children love this chair. It provides a feeling of privacy, safety, and fun.

- Use pop-up tents and tunnels.

- Use several great, inexpensive items, which Ikea also sells, to create whimsy and privacy: a large, polyester green leaf called Löva, which can be wall-mounted; a machine-washable white net canopy called Bryne; and a circus-themed, light-blue canopy called Mysig.

- Provide children with yards of sheer fabric, clothespins, and rope, and help them make their very own temporary sweet spots.

- Use carpet samples to make squares for sitting on. They're very inexpensive and sometimes free, and they can quickly create personal spaces for use during group time.

- Use hula hoops to create a perimeter for private space. For example, if a child needs time alone to play, you might place the

hoop and a toy or two around her and instruct the other children to stay out of her hoop, or private spot. These hoops are also useful when you are trying to organize a group of young children. I invite children to hold on to the hoop when it's group time, and they quickly cooperate.

- Use masking or duct tape to form squares on the floor or carpet, creating private spots.
- During outdoor play, use chalk to draw spaces on the asphalt or concrete.

Suggestion   Because safety is always an issue, only semiprivate spaces should be provided.

3

Smell the Flower, Blow Out the Candles

Purpose

To help children develop breath awareness

Materials   Collection of artificial flowers—or real ones!

Procedure   Hand out one flower to each child. One hand should hold the flower, and the other should be held up, fingers spread, to form pretend candles on a cake. Put your nose next to the flower in your hand, and take a slow, deep breath through your nose, pretending to smell the flower. Say, "Smell the flower" as you breathe in deeply through your nose. Then say, "Blow out the birthday candles" as you blow onto each of your fingers through your mouth.

Assist the children in doing the same. After a while, they won't need their flowers to breathe deeply. This activity makes things go more smoothly during transitions between activities.

4

Fun with Feathers

Purpose

To help children develop breath awareness

Materials Feathers

Procedure Play this early American party game in which children try to see who can keep their feathers afloat the longest by blowing on them. Check to make sure there are no known allergies to feathers.

At group time, let children select feathers to hold in their hands while they practice deep, long breathing. They can see and feel the effect of their breathing when the feathers move.

5 Tummy Toys

Purpose

To help children develop breath awareness

Materials   A collection of small stuffed toys

Procedure   In a large-group setting, ask the children to place small stuffed toys on their tummies. Explain that this is a quiet time, and turn down the lights while keeping outside disturbances to a minimum. Practice slow, deep breathing, and ask the children to watch as their toys slowly rise and then fall. Don't be surprised if they fall asleep!

6

Bunny Breathing

Purpose

To help children develop breath awareness

Materials None

Procedure Ask the children if they have ever noticed how a bunny wrinkles up its nose when it breathes. Together, take short, quick in-breaths through the nose three times, followed by a nice, long exhalation out the mouth while saying, "Haaaaaaaaaaah."

7

Pinwheels

Purpose

To help children learn breath awareness

Materials Simple pinwheels

Procedure Pass out a pinwheel to each child. Ask these questions:

- Can you make the wheel spin?

- What do you think is moving the wheel?

- Why is breathing important?

- Can you make the pinwheel move quickly? move slowly?

- Can you see your breath?

Children can experience the effect of their breathing when the pinwheel spins. Ask questions that help the children become aware of their breath.

8

Hoberman Sphere

Purpose

To help children learn breath awareness

Materials A Hoberman sphere, which is a structure resembling a geodesic dome. It can be folded down to a fraction of its normal size in a magical motion that mesmerizes adults and children. This visual really helps children learn breath awareness. Hoberman spheres are available online at Amazon and can be bought at Target and Walmart. They come in mega, mini, and micro sizes. For more information, visit www.hoberman.com/fold/Sphere/sphere.htm.

Procedure Take out the sphere, and use it as a prop during circle time to practice deep breathing. You can also use it with individual children. As you breathe in, expand the sphere, and as you exhale, contract the sphere. The action really helps children learn breath awareness and create calm. Don't let the fact that the toy isn't indestructible deter you from buying it.

9

Sensory Breathing Basket

Purpose

To create a collection of props that help children reduce stress and make quiet time part of each day

Materials Feathers, Hoberman sphere, plastic flowers (one for each child), squishy balls, small soft toys, pinwheels, bubblers, books related to breathing and calm

Procedure Fill a basket with as many of the items as possible. I like to use clear plastic bags to keep the items in the basket organized. Pull out the collection during circle time, and conduct a breath awareness or sensory activity.

Read *Shhh . . .* by Guido van Genechten (2001)

10

"Quiet Peaceful"

Purpose

To help children learn how to calm themselves

Materials   The song "Quiet Peaceful"

Procedure   Sing "Quiet Peaceful" with the children, using the accompanying movements so that they associate calming with specific actions

"Quiet Peaceful" by Judith Anne Rice

Breathe in, breathe out.
Sometimes it's best to take a rest.
Quiet, peaceful [*alternate resting cheek on folded hands*],
Calm your body down [*rub tummy*].
Shhhhhh. . . [*place one finger on your lips*].

Like a baby [*pretend to cradle a baby*],
On a fluffy cloud of love.
Quiet, peaceful [*alternate resting cheek on folded hands*],
Calm your body down [*rub your tummy*].
Shhhhhh. . . [*place one finger on your lips*].

Like a feather [*move your fingers like feathers floating*],
Floating on a sea of air.
Quiet, peaceful [*alternate resting cheek on folded hands*],
Calm your body down [*rub your tummy*].
Shhhhhh. . . [*place one finger on your lips*].

Relax, let go [*lift and hold your shoulders next to your ears; then let them drop*],
Sometimes it's best to take a rest.
Quiet, peaceful [*alternate resting cheek on each folded hand*],
Calm your body down [*rub your tummy*].
Shhhhhh. . . [*place one finger on your lips*].

Suggestion   View a video demonstration of the song at www.JudithAnneRice
.com.

Read   *Each Breath a Smile* by Sister Susan (2001)

11

Yoga for Young Children

Purpose

To help children develop coordination, balance, attention span, flexibility, self-regulation, awareness, and relaxation, all of which are antidotes to stress

Materials

Timer, yoga books and programs that teach yoga to children, such as the following:

Yoga Motion (DVD) by NamasteKid.com

Yoga Calm for Children: Educating Heart, Mind, and Body by Lynea and Jim Gillen (2007) (YogaCalm.org also presents a training program for teaching yoga to young children.)

Calm-Down Time by Elizabeth Verdick (2010)

Itsy Bitsy Yoga for Toddlers and Preschoolers: 8-Minute Routines to Help Your Child Grow Smarter, Be Happier, and Behave Better by Helen Garabedian (2008)

Little Yoga: A Toddler's First Book of Yoga by Rebecca Whitford (2005)

Peaceful Piggy Meditation by Kerry Lee MacLean (2004)

Yoga Kit for Kids by Imaginazium, www.imaginazium.com

You can find free yoga videos online. Other online videos have monthly fees or fees to download them onto your computer.

Procedure

Start by practicing stillness. In large group, ask the children if they can pretend to be a quiet little mouse, turtle, or some other favorite character for just thirty seconds. Then set a timer. Praise the children who succeed at maintaining stillness. Slowly add more time.

The best way to introduce the poses is one at a time, with pictures and demonstrations. Work up to five or six. The poses develop coordination, balance, attention span, and flexibility. Start out slowly, doing poses for only five to ten minutes. At first, yoga can be frustrating for children because most of them are not familiar with it. With practice, they will begin to look forward to it, and you will be amazed at how cooperative and skilled young children can become. Eventually, you can add more time to each pose.

12

Freshersize

Purpose

To increase the amount of time children spend freely outdoors

Materials Various

Procedure Here are some ways to have fun "freshersizing":

- Set up pop-up tents to make an instant campground for dramatic outdoor play.
- Observe the weather.
- Spend time outdoors in all sorts of weather. Dressing and undressing a group of preschoolers in their winter gear can be a huge job, but the pros far outweigh the cons—so go for it!

Children do not have to have a fancy play area with a lot of equipment. They love to dig, poke, haul, collect, chase, and discover on their own.

Suggestions If nothing else, remember that when preschool children dance in rain, jump in leaves, listen to snow crunch underfoot, immerse hands inside slimy pumpkins, pet rabbits, and smell the earth while it's awakening in spring, they are experiencing the physical world firsthand. This is how the world comes to life for them and how they come to life.

Go to www.JudithAnneRice.com to watch the video *The Power of Rest!*

13

Connecting with Nature

Purpose

To familiarize children with the natural world

Materials   Various

Procedure   A curriculum that includes nature as part of its framework is all-inclusive and provides a path to connecting with the natural world. Use these ideas to connect children with nature:

- Freshersize. Get outside and play.

- Start a nature journal, keeping track of kids' observations in writings and pictures.

- Go on a bird-watching hike. Make pretend binoculars out of recycled cardboard tubes taped together, and add yarn with a hole punch. Bring along a real, quality pair of binoculars so the children can take turns using them. Record your observations in the nature journal.

- Read *It Looked Like Spilt Milk* by Charles G. Shaw (1988). Bring a camera outside, and take photos of clouds the children have noticed. Then ask them to describe what the clouds look like. Use the photos to make a cloud collage display.

- Bring a bug house outside so the children can practice a catch-and-release bug game.

- Ask community volunteers to keep the outdoor play area clean and free of litter.

- Move indoor activities, like easel painting, story time, snack, dance, and music, outdoors when weather permits.

- Celebrate the changing seasons.

- Go on field trips to open spaces, campgrounds, parks, zoos, gardens, farms, lakes, and beaches. A parent once opened up her garden to my class and gave us a tour while she shared her vast knowledge of nature. Then she gave all of the children their own plant.

- Name and adopt a tree outside of the classroom window. Take photos of it in fall, winter, and spring, and put those photos in a nature journal. In the fall, make bookmarkers and leaf rubbings. In the winter, make bird feeders and observe the birds. At the end of winter, count the days until the buds burst, and then celebrate spring. On warm days, hold story time under the shade of the tree. Record and place all of the changes that the children observe into the nature journal.

- Add a fish bowl to your space. Watching fish in an aquarium can decrease blood pressure.

- Expand your sensory play by replacing the usual water or sand with some of these items in the water table:

a collection of river rocks	
goldfish	spring blossoms
milkweeds	cattails
birdseed (no peanuts)	feathers
snow	seashells
leaves	cedar chips
pinecones	tree branches
grasses	various types of bark

- Add live plants to your space.

- Collect rainwater for indoor and outdoor plants.

- Instead of heavy bags of potting soil, use peat pellets (available at garden centers) to start flowers, vegetables, and plants. The children can transplant them to a larger container or outside after the plants mature.

- Try to get people from the community to bring in unusual animals or pets for a visit, and talk about the attention and care that animals need.

- Plant a butterfly garden in a sunny location (five to six hours of sun each day) sheltered from the wind. Butterflies need the sun to warm them, but they won't want to feed in an area where they are constantly fighting the wind to stay on the plants. Place a few flat stones in your sunny location so the butterflies can take a break while warming up.

- Butterflies need water, just as we do. Keep a mud puddle damp in a sunny location, or fill a bucket with sand and enough water to make the sand moist.

- Do not use pesticides in your garden. Butterflies use two different types of plants—those that provide nectar for the adults to eat (nectar plant) and those that provide food for their offspring (host plant). Find out which plant species are native to your area. To learn more about butterfly gardening, visit www.butterflywebsite.com.

- Add a birdbath to your outdoor space. A birdbath is a strong attraction for birds, especially during droughts. Birdbaths that offer a reliable source of water in winter can add to this attraction. A very shallow, gradually deepening birdbath that is safe from cats, kept clean, and refreshed frequently with clean water to avoid contamination and mosquitoes can attract many different species of birds. Two inches of water in the center are all that is needed for most backyard birds because they do not submerge their bodies, only dip their wings to splash water on their backs. Elevation is a common safety measure, providing a clear area around the birdbath free from hidden predators. The birdbath will attract more birds if it's placed where a frightened bird can easily fly to an overhanging limb or resting place if disturbed or attacked.

- On a nature walk, ask the children to collect flowers, leaves, and grasses. Ask them to secure their treasures on the sticky side of a seven-inch strip of masking tape. Then cover the sticky side of the tape with the sticky side of another seven-inch strip of masking tape. Make nature bracelets by gently wrapping the tape around the children's wrists and connecting the two ends with a small, third piece of tape.

Suggestion Be sure to check for children who may be allergic to any of your sensory play materials.

Chapter 2  Love

Kindness in words creates confidence. Kindness in thinking creates profoundness.
Kindness in giving creates love.
—Lao Tzu (600 BC), Chinese philosopher, father of Taoism

Defining love precisely is difficult because by its very nature love occurs in many forms. Among these are romantic love, the love that we feel toward family and friends, and universal love, such as the love we feel for all humankind. For the purpose of educating young children, a useful definition of love is "an unselfish and benevolent concern for the good of others." Throughout our lives, love remains priceless and is the key to our happiness and well-being. According to Barbara Coloroso, children who bully are likely to come from homes where love is conditional: parents only love the child under certain conditions rather than steadily, always, and without regard for the child's behavior.

Unfortunately, children's understanding of love is often built on what they observe of unhealthy adult relationships at home or in the powerful public media. Some children are raised in abusive homes where one partner or both partners turn repeatedly to violence in their relationship. The abused partner reasons that the other partner "really does love me and the kids." The messages children in such families receive are that people who love each other hit each other and that violence is acceptable. Even when physical violence isn't present at home, many children live with adults who equate love with emotional storms. Desperately in love is not, in fact, love at all; rather, it is desperately dependent.

Television, movies, and magazines often confuse love with manipulation, lying, cheating, sex, and violence. I believe that much of the staggering increase in teenage pregnancy, violence, and drug and alcohol abuse is due to modern society's distorted definitions of love.

Some of the erroneous but commonly held beliefs, conscious and unconscious, that define love and how to get it can be understood through equations.

Abuse + Denial = Love	Refusal to recognize the lack of love
Alcohol + Drugs = Love	Addictions take the place of love
Mom + Dad + Hitting = Love	Children learn battering is part of love
Teenagers + Sex = Love	Responsibility is ignored in the name of love
Control + Dependency = Love	Unhealthy domination and reliance are thought to be love
Belonging + Rebellion = Love	Gangs appear to provide love

Healthy people do not buy into these equations. They can plainly see that two plus two does not equal six. Those who do hold these views find that their need for love remains unsatisfied; they are looking for it in all the wrong places. We must learn and teach that love is kind, patient, unconditional, forgiving, trusting, tender, unselfish, and lasting. We must learn and teach that love comes from within, not from without.

Help children develop healthy belief systems about love and learn how to experience it throughout their lives by modeling love in the classroom. Teach children ways to express their love for themselves, one another, their families, and their communities. For some children, the love you offer may be most of the love they receive during their precious childhood years, affecting them for the rest of their lives.

1

Love Poster

Purpose

To help reinforce a healthy definition of love for children

Materials   Construction paper, copier paper, black marker, glue, other decoration materials

Procedure   A simple definition of love is "an unselfish and kindhearted concern for the good of others and for ourselves." Run off copies of the definition, and cut them into strips. Trace both of each child's hands on white construction paper, and cut them out, creating a beak shape at the tip of each thumb (this will be the dove's head). Glue the hand shapes on a piece of colored construction paper, thumbs facing one another. They should look like two doves after you add a black dot for an eye on each one. Place another piece of paper, this one shaped like a heart, between the two birds. Glue the definition of love to the bottom of each sheet. The children can add other details. Send the Love Poster home with the children to share with their parents. After all, we all need to be reminded of what real love is.

2

Acts of Kindness

Purpose

To acknowledge, value, and reinforce positive things children have done; to help them develop a sense of compassion and connection with other people

Materials   None

Procedure   Ask children to share a recent kind deed they did for someone else. For example, "I helped my little sister pick up her toys." "I shared my teddy with my friend Lily." "I stopped my little brother from crossing the street." Give a round of applause for each act of kindness.

Read   *Little Miss Spider at Sunny Patch School* by David Kirk (2000)

3

Kindness Coupon Book

Purpose

To help children learn the practice of giving nonmaterial gifts to others

Materials   Kindness coupon book (appendix A, pages 134–35), one for each child; crayons or markers; scissors

Procedure   Discuss the idea that we can give others very important gifts that do not cost money, such as sharing toys, helping a parent set the table, or cheering up a sad friend. Give children their own coupon book to fold, color, and take home to their parents. Explain that when their parents give them a coupon, their job is to do what the coupon says. For example, if they receive the "15 minutes of quiet play" coupon, they must play quietly for fifteen minutes.

Note: This activity works best with four- and five-year-olds, but families can use the books with younger children as introductions to the concept of nonmaterial gifts.

4

Pennies from Heaven

Materials   A large, empty container with a lid, such as a five-gallon ice-cream pail with a slot cut in the lid, a piggy bank, or a coffee can; old magazines; scissors; tape; crayons or markers

Procedure   Talk to the children about their concerns for their school, neighborhood, or city. Perhaps they want to replace a piece of worn-out playground equipment. Maybe they are worried about the homeless people they see.

Suggest that the class collect money for one of these causes. You may want to designate Friday as "Penny Day" and encourage the children to bring a penny or two from home on that day. Ask the children to help decorate the empty container, attaching cutout pictures from magazines to remind them why they are saving money.

After the last "Penny Day," explain that you will now use the money to fulfill the purpose. On a subsequent day, conduct an awards ceremony, present the gift, and celebrate the class's accomplishment.

Suggestion   Conduct a premath activity by having the children count out the pennies in groups of five or ten, depending on their skills.

Read   *I Am Generous!* by David Parker (2004)

5

Kiss Pictures

Purpose

To help children share a symbol of affection with someone they love

Materials Blank face picture (appendix A, page 136), one for each child; markers or crayons; mirrors; tissue paper; lipstick (ask each child to bring an old tube; keep extra samples from an Avon or Mary Kay distributor on hand)

Procedure Ask children to use the markers or crayons to draw a picture of their face, omitting the mouth, on the blank face picture. Tell the children to apply some lipstick to their lips and to kiss the picture on the spot where the mouth should be. The picture is complete. Encourage the children to take the pictures home and give them to loved ones.

Suggestion For sanitary purposes, make sure the children do not share lipstick. Ask the children to use mirrors when applying the lipstick to help them keep the makeup on their lips.

Read *The I Love You Book* by Todd Parr (2009)

6

The Kindness Pledge

Purpose

To teach children a ritual that reinforces kindness at home and in the classroom

Materials   None

Procedure   At the beginning of every class, ask the children to stand, raise their right hands, and recite this pledge:

I will be kind on this day and think good thoughts along the way.

Read   *Little Miss Spider at Sunny Patch School* by David Kirk (2000) and *The Peace Book* by Todd Parr (2004)

7

Gifts

Purpose

To help children experience the joy of creating and giving gifts

Materials Various

Procedure These are easy-to-make gifts children can make and give away. For almost limitless great ideas, go to FamilyFun.com. It's a great website with tons of recipes, seasonal crafts, cards and gifts, how-to videos, and fun everyday ideas.

- Stationery: You'll need plain, white envelopes; copier paper; decorative rubber stamps and ink; colorful strips of ribbon; and tape. Ask each child to decorate three sheets of paper and three envelopes. Fold each sheet in half and slide it under an envelope flap. Help the children tape a colorful ribbon around their new stationery.

- Seasonal book markers: You'll need clear contact paper cut into six-by-nine-inch pieces and a variety of items, depending on the season. Here are some suggestions:

    in fall, colorful leaves collected on a neighborhood walk
    in winter, cut-up white doilies, glitter, cutout holiday cards
    in spring, lilacs, apple blossoms, grass, various flower petals
    in summer, green leaves, sand, wildflowers

- Prepare the contact paper by peeling back the top layer halfway from the long side. Ask the children to arrange the objects on the exposed sticky surface. After their arrangement is complete, help them peel back the rest of the contact paper and fold the sticky sides together.

Read *The Giving Tree* by Shel Silverstein (1964), *Giving* by Shirley Hughes (2005), and *Feeling Thankful* by Shelley Rotner (2000)

8

The Peace Project

Purpose

To help children learn ways to create peace

Materials *The Peace Book* by Todd Parr (2004)

Procedure Read the book to the children; then choose pages from the book to turn into peace projects. Here are some examples:

Peace is making new friends. Ask the children to make a new friend that day.

Peace is planting a tree. Plant a tree together.

Peace is learning another language. Practice saying "hello" in several languages.

Peace is wearing different clothes. Ask the children to dress differently one day.

Peace is having enough pizza in the world for everyone. Collect change to donate to a food shelter.

Peace is new babies being born. Invite a parent to visit the children with a new baby.

Peace is keeping someone warm. Collect mittens for a shelter.

Peace is wishing on a star. Write down children's individual wishes on construction paper stars. The children can decorate their star wishes and then hang them from the ceiling.

Encourage the children to think about what peace is and how they can make peace!

Chapter 3   Feelings and Empathy

I believe that empathy is the most essential quality of civilization.
—Roger Ebert

Empathy is the ability to understand the feelings and experiences of others without their telling us. Although it might seem that young children aren't yet capable of empathy, anyone who observes them closely knows they can acquire basic perspective-taking skills. During their preschool years, most children begin to recognize the six emotions of happiness, sadness, anger, surprise, fear, and silliness. The awareness of these feelings gives them the basis for improving their empathy skills.

Anger, jealously, and fear are all part of the human experience. Children experience these feelings. If those are acknowledged and used for solving problems, they can be beneficial; if they are repressed, they can cause bigger problems. One of the most interesting books I have read is *The Divided Mind: The Epidemic of Mindbody Disorders* by John E. Sarno (2006), who believes that more often than not, back and neck pain, ulcers, colitis, tension headaches, and many other painful disorders are due to repressed emotions.

If this is true and bad feelings translate into physical ailments, how can you help children express all kinds of feelings rather than bottle them up and embody them? Here are a few ways:

- Tell children it's okay to get angry, but they cannot hurt other people or break things.
- Allow children to express anger by pounding wooden pegs or playdough, tearing up paper (pretending to be a human shredding machine), breaking wooden craft sticks, jumping on a mini-trampoline, throwing balls, bellowing Tarzan calls, and blasting off steam in other safe ways.

- Teach the names of emotions so children can begin to communicate their feelings.

- Listen to what children have to say or contribute.

- Within limits, give children who bite something they can bite, like a teething ring. They can carry it around with them in a pocket or use a pacifier clip to hook it onto their clothes. Give children who hit something they can hit. Let children who yell, yell. Give them a time and place. Let children who fidget fidget. Give them something they can play with (a squishy ball to squeeze) while continuing to participate in the group.

- Give children enough physical free-play time to help them release tension.

- Encourage children to assert themselves. If a child says someone hit her, ask her to tell that person in a big, strong voice, "Stop! Do not hit me! That makes me mad!"

- Help children feel validated by acknowledging their feelings. Together you can make wishes, visualize a happier time, write down feelings in a letter, or paint a picture. You can give them hugs, hope, and support to help them cope with tough situations.

- Give children permission to experience their feelings. Say, "It's okay to cry. Would you like a tissue or a teddy bear to hold?"

- Make sure your reaction to their anger or tantrum is one of acceptance. Allow them to express feelings safely without trying to stop them. Give them permission by saying, "It looks like you are really feeling angry. Maybe you could go over to the rug or pound a pillow so you don't get hurt."

- Sometimes children begin to identify with who they are by equating themselves with their feelings, such as "I am shy" or "I am a naughty kid." Feelings are neither good nor bad; they come and go. Remind these children, "You are [child's name]. Sometimes you may feel [shy, naughty, etc.], but that is not who you are." Sit down with them and make a list of some of their qualities, which is a good way to make the discussion more concrete.

- When a child is making a bad choice, rewind and give him the chance to start over. Say, "Let's try this again. What would be a better choice?"

- Write down the problem on a piece of paper to acknowledge it, and then have the child tear up the paper to express anger.

For children to develop empathy, they need to recognize several things, such as

- Knowing how other people feel—and caring about them—will help children make and keep friends.

- It's okay when others do not feel the same way they do. Often young children feel bad when a playmate does not want to play with them. Reassure them that they should not take the action personally and that the two can still be friends.

- Feelings can change. Explain to children that it's normal for them to be happy one day and sad the next.

- When talking to other people, they should stop what they're doing, look into the other's eyes (culture permitting), and listen.

- "I" messages help us communicate. With practice, children will be able to give "I" messages on their own.

- Some actions are done on purpose, and others are accidental. By three years of age, most children understand that some actions are intentional and others are unintentional. Nonetheless, they *feel* that most acts are deliberate. When one child is upset because of the accidental action of another and perceives it as intentional, bring the two together to talk about what happened. During the conversation, explain the difference between "on purpose" and "accidental."

If a child resists communication, I kneel down and say, "Look into my eyes so I know you can hear what I have to say."

Show the children how to communicate, and help them practice appropriate ways to respond. Always praise their behavior when they express understanding and concern or when they offer help to their playmates.

1

Feelings Lotto

Purpose

To help children learn the names of feelings and remind them that they should ask for help when they are feeling unsafe

Materials   Six feeling faces (appendix A, page 137), clear contact paper, construction paper

Procedure   Most children cannot tell you how they feel because they do not know the names of their feelings. This activity will familiarize them with those names and improve communication skills. The six feeling faces can be used in three ways:

1. Give each child one sheet of faces. Cut up other sheets, distribute a mix of individual feelings cards to the children, and play a lotto game.

2. Cut out pairs of each feeling, mount them on construction paper, laminate or cover with clear contact paper, and use them to play Concentration.

3. Use the page as a tool to help children clarify how they feel. Ask, "Which face looks like how you feel?" and then encourage them to circle and color that face. Discuss.

Read   *Llama Llama Red Pajama* by Anna Dewdney (2005), *It's Okay to Be Different* by Todd Parr (2001), *The I'm Not Scared Book* by Todd Parr (2011), *The Feelings Book* by Todd Parr (2005), and *On Monday When It Rained* by Cherryl Kachenmeister (1989)

Note: *The Three Bears* by Byron Barton (1991) is a delight. After you read the story, ask the children, "How did Baby Bear feel when he found his chair broken? How did Goldilocks feel when she woke up and saw three bears looking at her?" Explore the feelings of the characters in other stories that the children are familiar with.

2 Friendship Bracelets

To help children practice trading and strengthen their friendships

Materials Baker's clay (two cups flour, one cup salt, enough water to form a dough consistency), plastic straws, tempera paint, small brushes, string or yarn

Procedure Have the children form small beads with the clay and push a plastic straw through each one to make a hole. Allow the beads to air dry for at least two days. When dry, paint the beads, using small brushes to get more detail. When the paint has dried, ask the children to exchange beads until everyone has a new set of beads. String the beads on the yarn to create friendship bracelets.

Suggestion If some children are reluctant to trade their beads, don't push them to do so. Reinforce the behavior of those who have traded their beads, and encourage the others to join in.

3

The Professor Smarty Show

Purpose

To help children practice perspective-taking and thinking skills, which reinforce empathy

Materials Toy microphone, two chairs, list of questions (some suggestions):

What would you do if a friend fell down?

If someone painted a beautiful picture, how do you think he might feel?

If someone grabbed a toy from you, how would you feel?

What could you do if a new child came to school and did not know where the bathroom was?

What could you do if someone was feeling lonely and didn't have anyone to play with?

How would a friend feel if she lost a favorite toy?

Procedure The success of this activity depends on your ability to dramatize a television game show in which the children are the contestants. Seat the children on the floor in front of your chair, and place another chair at your side. Explain that you are all going to pretend to be on the "Professor Smarty Show."

Ask one child at a time to come up on stage and sit in the chair. Introduce the child by saying something like, "Welcome to the Professor Smarty Show. What is your name?" Use the microphone to interview each contestant, and ask him one of your questions. If the child cannot answer, someone in the audience can try. The children should applaud when a contestant takes the stage and when he returns to the audience.

Suggestion   Use this fun game to help children gain knowledge or skills on almost any topic.

Read   *Everybody Has Feelings* by Charles E. Avery (1998). This book depicts the moods of children and uses English and Spanish text.

4   "I" Messages

Purpose

To help children learn about, create, and reinforce "I" messages

Materials   None

Procedure   "I" messages are sentences that begin with the pronoun "I" instead of "you." Because they state the feelings or needs of the speaker, "I" messages promote empathy. They enable children to understand their own feelings and those of their friends. "You" messages often sound negative and tend to block communication, while "I" messages communicate in a positive way.

Help the children practice turning "You" messages into "I" messages. At first they will need help identifying their feelings and the reasons for those feelings. You will also have to help them construct their "I" messages. With enough practice and modeling, they will begin to use "I" messages on their own. Here are some examples:

"You hit me" becomes "I feel angry when you hit me."

"You are supposed to share" changes to "I would like a turn."

"You knocked down my castle" becomes "I feel sad because my castle is wrecked."

5

Dolly Hospital

Purpose

To give children opportunities to act out caring for others in dramatic play

Materials   Doctor's kit and hospital props, such as stethoscopes, white coats, and bandages

Procedure   Set up a hospital in your dramatic play area. Dolls and kids can be the patients. Supply plenty of doctor's kits and bandages for boo-boos. See if you can obtain some old X-rays for displays.

6 Cheerleader Pom-poms

Purpose

To help children create and use a prop that encourages others to succeed

Materials Newspaper, ruler, scissors, masking tape, tempera paint, paintbrushes

Procedure If colored pom-poms are desired, ask the children to first paint sheets of newspaper and let them dry. Close the paper on its natural crease, and draw horizontal lines two inches apart, starting at the open edge of the paper and ending two inches before reaching the fold. Have the children cut along the lines. When they are finished, tightly roll the fold from end to end. Then wrap with masking tape, forming a handle for the pom-pom.

The pom-poms can be used to cheer on fellow classmates during relay races. Cheering, jumping, and waving the pom-poms are usually enough, but you can make the exercise more authentic. Here's a pom-pom cheer:

Go [child's name]! Go!
Go [child's name]! Go!
You can do it. That we know!

7

Pom-pom Relays

Purpose

To help children have fun while they encourage and support others

Materials   Pom-poms from activity 6, objects to use in relay races

Procedure   Explain to the children that it's important to encourage others to succeed. While one child or group tries to do something, the others act as cheerleaders. The activities themselves are secondary—the focus here should be on the children who are cheering. Show them the joys and positive effects of cooperatively supporting others. Here are some sample relays:

- Form a bucket brigade to fill the water table.

- Rake leaves across the grass in fall to form a pile.

- Hold an open umbrella over your head, and walk an imaginary tightrope (made by putting tape on the floor).

- Blow bubbles or a feather across the room.

- Carry a Ping-Pong ball in a large spoon across the room.

- Balance a feather on your head, and walk across the room.

- Cut out large sheets of blue paper and lay them across the room (be sure to tape them down) for relay puddle jumping.

Read   *Caps for Sale: A Tale of a Peddler, Some Monkeys, and Their Monkey Business* by Esphyr Slobodkina (1968); then balance several caps on each child's head, and ask them to walk across the room without dropping the caps.

8

Stompers

Purpose

To teach children an appropriate outlet for their anger

Materials   Empty rectangular tissue boxes, paint, brushes, duct tape, scissors

Procedure   Reinforce and size the opening of the tissue boxes with duct tape so children can wear them like slippers. Ask children to paint their stompers like monster feet. Use them after a discussion about getting mad: "It's okay to be angry, but don't hurt other people." Children can pretend to be big, strong elephants, dinosaurs, or monsters, and stomp their big, strong feet! Sing, "If you're happy and you know it" and change the words to "If you're angry and you know it, stomp your feet—stomp—stomp!"

Read   *If You're Angry and You Know It!* by Cecily Kaiser (2004) and *Cool Down and Work Through Anger* by Cheri J. Meiners (2010)

9

Boo-boo Band-Aids

Purpose

To help children discover ways to comfort themselves and others

Materials   Empty (preferably metal) Band-Aid container, flesh-toned construction paper cut out to look like Band-Aids, markers

Procedure   Talk to the children about what they can do when someone gets hurt or is feeling sad. Work together to think of ways to comfort a hurting friend. Some ideas include

- saying, "Sorry you are sad"
- giving a hug
- passing a tissue
- offering a snuggly blanket

Write the children's ideas on the Band-Aids. Then when someone is hurting, get out the container and help the hurting child choose the Boo-boo Band-Aid that best suits the situation. Bystanders can then do whatever the Band-Aid suggests to help the hurt child.

10

Homemade Stress Toys

Purpose

To help children identify emotions and give them a tool for reducing stress

Materials   Balloons, flour, empty plastic water bottle, small plastic funnel, permanent markers

Procedure   Using the funnel, fill the empty plastic water bottle with flour. Attach the end of a balloon to the top of the bottle. Turn the bottle upside down and squeeze gently to fill the balloon to the size of a tennis ball. Fill six balloons, tie them off, and draw one of the six feeling faces (see appendix A, page 137) on each balloon. Children can identify the feelings and manipulate the balloons to relieve stress.

Suggestion   A variety of inexpensive stress toys can be purchased from orientaltrading.com.

Read   *Cool Down and Work Through Anger* by Cheri J. Meiners (2010)

11

Owl Babies

Purpose

To alleviate children's separation anxiety

Materials Brown paper lunch bags, cupcake liners, markers, glue, feathers, precut construction paper triangles, *Owl Babies* by Martin Waddell (1996)

Procedure When children first arrive at a child care center, family child care home, or school, they normally feel a lot of separation anxiety. I have found that reciting the poem "Mommy Came Back," reading *Owl Babies,* and asking the children to act out the story with owl puppets they make help them process their fears and feelings about separation. Here is the poem:

"Mommy Came Back" by Judith Anne Rice
  [*you can vary* Mommy *with other family members*]

Three little owls sitting in a tree,
The first one said, "Where's our Mommy?"
The second one said, "She's got things to do."
And the third one said, "She'll come back when she's through."

Twinkle went the stars in the dark quiet night [*mimic twinkling stars*],
Then Mommy came back and hugged them tight [*children hug themselves*].

The children can make owl puppets by drawing eyes in the centers of two cupcake liners and gluing them onto a brown paper lunch bag, then gluing on two triangles for ears and one for a beak. Finally, add feathers, and use as a puppet.

12 IWantItNow Monsters

Purpose

To help children learn to delay gratification and deal with frustration positively

Materials Paper grocery bags, scissors, art scraps, markers, glue, small bean bags

Procedure Children who consistently get what they want often end up never feeling satisfied. At those moments when a young child wants something strongly but either must wait to get it or go without it, you should always acknowledge her feelings. A good way to respond is to say, "It sounds like you really want that ___." Then talk to the child about what she can do while she either waits or goes without. Here are several ways to help children deal with the *I want it now!* feeling:

- Ask them to draw a picture of what they want. This distracts, calms, and clarifies.

- Let them make a wish with a wishing wand.

- Use the kid cards in appendix A, page 140–43, for calming or expressing anger.

- Let them know they can have a big, fat tantrum if they need to.

- Encourage them to make and feed an IWantItNow Monster.

Use two grocery bags, one tucked upside down within the other to form a cube, to make the IWantItNow Monster. Ask the children to draw a face on one side. Then cut out a large mouth and decorate it with art scraps. Children can feed the IWantItNow Monster by throwing bean bags into its mouth to deal with their *I want it now!* feeling.

Read *I Just Don't Like the Sound of No!* by Julia Cook (2011)

13

Make Yourself Happy

Purpose

To help children learn ways to be happy

Materials Large circular paper cutouts (approximately nine inches in diameter), crayons, tape, life-size drawing of a clown

Procedure In a large circle, ask the children, "What is your favorite way to make yourself happy?" List the responses on a large sheet of paper. (Even though the children cannot read, writing down their words validates their thoughts.)

Next, ask the children to each draw a picture on a circle of their favorite way to make themselves happy. When finished, children can tape their circles onto the clown's suit. Later, when a child seems unhappy, you can refer him to his circle.

Encourage children to do things that they have control over, for example, tickle their toes, sing, dance, build a fort, work a puzzle, look at a favorite book, hug their snuggliest toys, make a new friend, play an instrument, or draw a beautiful picture. Assist them in thinking happy thoughts, like watching the first snowfall, petting a puppy, picking dandelions, and eating homemade spaghetti!

This activity can help children develop inner control over their own happiness, lessening their dependence on things beyond their control. The resulting resiliency makes them less vulnerable to loneliness and sadness.

Read *The Feel Good Book* by Todd Parr (2002) and *The Happy Book* by Diane Muldrow (1999)

Chapter 4 Gentleness

Nothing is so strong as gentleness, nothing so gentle as real strength.
—Apples of Gold

Gentleness is the acting out of love. Children must experience gentleness in order to feel loved, and must practice gentleness in order to love others. Ideally, children learn to apply gentleness to their physical actions and emotions.

A growing body of research tells us of the incredible effects of gentle touch on human beings. Tiffany Field and her colleagues at the Touch Research Institute at the University of Miami School of Medicine found that premature babies who were massaged increased in weight and development more than preemies who were not massaged (Cohen 1994). In another study led by Field (2006), children in a psychiatric unit who received a series of massages not only felt and slept better but also showed a decrease in the levels of hormones associated with anxiety.

Teachers are not massage therapists or nurses, but they can give a comforting hand squeeze, a gentle pat on the back, or a reassuring hug, all of which are effective ways to relieve separation anxiety, calm tantrums, and provide comfort to a lonely or sad child. You can also model gentleness in your tone of voice and direct physical contact with the children. Touching children's hands, heads, or shoulder can help them feel welcome when they first arrive at school as well as cared about

when they leave for home. Simple, appropriate, gentle touch can demonstrate approval, help build self-esteem, and create a sense of belonging, security, and healing.

Because of today's hurried lifestyles, many children and adults spend little time engaging in the quiet, gentle activities that help human beings establish inner peace and form positive connections with others. When you name gentleness and introduce young children to gentle acts, you give them the concrete experiences they need to understand and develop gentle behavior. For some children, the activities in this chapter may be their only opportunities to experience and apply the gentleness that is so helpful to their own well-being.

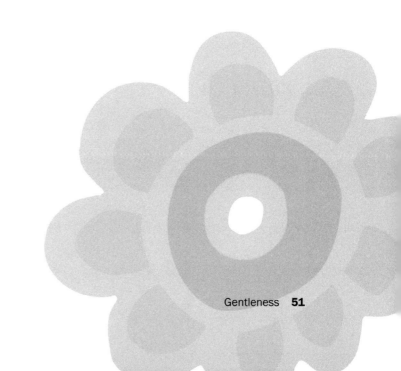

1

Bathing Babies

Purpose

To help children practice gentleness and observe the gentle interaction between a parent and infant

Materials Photographs of the children as babies; water table with warm, soapy water; towels; soap; dolls that can be bathed; doll clothing; toy baby bottles. A parent with an infant!

Procedure A few days before this activity, collect photos from the children of themselves when they were babies. Discuss the photos with them, and encourage the class to try to identify the babies. Ask if they can remember what it was like to be a baby. Do they have any baby brothers or sisters or know any babies? Ask them, "Do babies need to be treated in special ways?"

Invite a parent with an infant into the classroom to talk about how the baby is fed, clothed, and cared for. Ask the parent to demonstrate bathing the baby. Be sure the parent emphasizes that only adults can bathe real babies and that it is very important to be gentle, careful, and sometimes quiet with a baby.

Later in class, allow the children to feed (using toy baby bottles), clothe, and bathe the dolls. Fill the water table with a shallow amount of warm, soapy water. Provide small bars of soap, towels, and a place to dry and dress the dolls.

2

Feather Painting

Purpose

To help children learn gentleness and experience relaxation

Materials   Large, colorful feathers (purchased)

Procedure   Pair up the children, and ask them to sit across from one another. Tell them they are going to take turns pretending to paint each other in a very soft, gentle way, using a feather as a brush. Explain how important it is to not "paint" too close to their partner's eyes. Guide them in painting their partner's hair, cheeks, arms, and nose, and under his or her chin. Speak softly and slowly; turn the lights down. This is an amazingly calming and delightful activity.

Suggestion   Encourage the children to use a large feather as a paintbrush with tempera paint. Clean the feathers afterward by rinsing them with warm, soapy water and drying them.

3 Feather Play

Purpose

To give children opportunities to experiment with gentle touches

Materials Small, brightly colored feathers (purchased); various other materials

Procedure Use the feathers in the following ways:

- Fill the empty water table with feathers for a delightful sensory experience.

- Take one feather of each color, and tape each onto a separate paper plate. Hide the remaining feathers, and tell the children to find them. Have them sort the feathers according to color by putting each feather on the matching plate.

- Give each child one small feather. Play soft music, and ask the children to toss their feathers in the air and try to catch them.

- Play "Find the Bird" by having the children close their eyes while you place a trail of feathers that leads to a picture of a bird or to a small toy bird.

Read *The Quiet Book* by Deborah Underwood (2010)

4 Cake Decorating

Purpose

To give children a soft, gentle, creative experience

Materials Shaving cream, food coloring, several large plastic bowls, plastic knives, rubber spatulas, seasonal silk flowers and leaves

Procedure Fill two or more large bowls with shaving cream, and add a different food coloring to each one. Stir with a spatula to distribute color. Turn the bowls upside down to serve as pretend cakes. Allow the children to frost their cakes by spreading and smoothing the cream. Then they can decorate the cakes with the seasonal silk leaves and flowers, which can be rinsed, dried, and used over and over again.

5

Bubbles

Purpose

To help children develop the gentle skill of blowing bubbles

Materials Clean pail; one cup liquid dishwashing detergent (Joy or Dawn works best); three to four tablespoons glycerin from your pharmacy (optional); ten cups clean, cold water; large spoon; plastic bubble wands

Procedure Pour the water into the pail, and add the liquid detergent and the glycerin. (Glycerin makes the bubbles more durable.) Lightly stir, and then skim off any froth with the spoon. Distribute a plastic wand to each child, and demonstrate how to blow bubbles. Ask the children to blow their own bubbles and listen for any sound and observe how gently the bubbles float through the air and land softly. Point out that even when the bubbles burst, they do so quietly.

For outdoor play and something a little different, you can purchase some large bubble wands. Then set up a bubble obstacle course along a path. The children can blow their bubbles as they walk along the course. The path can require the children to blow a bubble through a hula hoop, walk backward, catch bubbles, and overcome other mild obstacles.

Suggestion A must for early-childhood activities is no-spill bubble tumblers, which are available from Little Kids (www.littlekidstoys.com), children's specialty stores, and Target.

6

The Power of Flour

Purpose

To help children engage in calming sensory play, using fine-motor, measuring, creative, and premath skills

Materials   Flour, measuring spoons and cups, funnels, bowls, plastic knives, cookie cutters, large sheets of paper (approximately the size of folded newspaper)

Procedure   Give children their own sheet of paper to use as a place mat. This defines their play space and makes cleanup easier. Also give each child a bowl of two to three cups of flour and an assortment of tools. Instruct the children to measure, pour, and play. The intensity with which the children engage in this activity will amaze you. Note how quiet the room becomes.

Note: Some teachers do not approve of using food for purposes other than eating. I use certain foods—flour, for example—that are inexpensive, natural, abundant, and reusable, making them excellent classroom materials. If you feel that your child and parent population would view the use of food for play as disturbing, honor their beliefs.

Jewel Floats

Purpose

To help children learn to make a calming toy they can use when they are stressed

Materials

Large, clear plastic pop bottles with caps; baby oil or water; food coloring (optional); waterproof tape; old jewelry; glitter; scraps of foil; small plastic toys

Procedure

The children can work in small groups or individually to create the jewel floats. Fill the pop bottles with baby oil or water; add coloring if you wish. Encourage the children to cut up foil scraps and drop them in their bottles. Add glitter, old jewelry, and small toys. Screw the caps securely on the bottles, and tape them closed.

When they turn the bottles upside down, the children can search for and track particular objects. Place the floats where they are accessible to the children in the room. Jewel floats are relaxing and soothing toys.

Suggestions

It's fun to create theme floats. For example, if the children are studying the ocean, a float can be filled with small shells, tiny plastic fish, and blue glitter. Adding only objects of the same color can create color themes.

Note: Whenever children are working with small pieces, they must be closely supervised because of the danger of choking if small pieces are put in the mouth.

8

Pussy Willow Pictures

Purpose

To help children use their hands gently and carefully

Materials   Pussy willows; light blue construction paper; brown crayons; gray tempera paint; two shallow pans, such as pie tins

Procedure   Allow the children to examine and touch a real pussy willow branch. Ask them to draw the branches on the paper, using brown crayons. Each child can then create the silky buds by dipping a finger into a shallow pan of gray paint and printing their fingerprint buds along the branches. This is a favorite springtime activity.

Read   *The Quiet Book* by Deborah Underwood (2010) and *Shhh . . .* by Guido van Genechten (2001)

Chapter 5 ✿ Respect

Do unto others as you would have them do unto you.
—The Golden Rule

At the center of a child's moral development lies respect. To become kindly and to be able to withstand the hurtful behavior of others, children need to learn to place a high value on themselves, others, and their environment. Perhaps the most effective way to teach children respect is to show them respect.

- Keep the rules simple: be nice to others, yourself, and personal belongings.
- Treat children like people, not cute little kiddies.
- Listen to them, even if you don't have the foggiest idea what they are talking about.
- Take their points of view into consideration. Include their thoughts in planning, problem solving, and setting limits.
- Provide them with explanations instead of "Because I said so."
- Act in a loving way.

Children need to learn to be comfortable saying "no" to a request and accepting "no" from someone else.

Another effective way to create respect in children is to help them recognize their personal relationships to others and to their surroundings. When they act responsibly toward other people and their possessions, their self-respect grows.

In our country we share ownership in many museums; zoos; recreation centers; schools; libraries; public roads; local, state, and national parks; and more. We also belong to the wider world of the human family and cultures. Children who grow up with a sense of belonging and an awareness of their ownership in society behave more respectfully and constructively.

In the classroom, children look surprised when I ask them, "Do you know who worked very hard to pay for all the toys and books we have in our room?" Then I say, "Your moms and dads and other people too!" The knowledge of their ownership (through their parents) seems to give them an increased appreciation and respect for the equipment they share.

At least once during every neighborhood walk, I dramatically point out to the children a piece of litter and say, "That makes me very sad." When they ask why I'm sad, I respond, "Someone didn't care about putting the trash where it belongs. That makes our neighborhood look messy. I know that you will remember to put trash where it belongs." The children really respond to this message. Parents have told me that they cannot go for a walk without bringing home a bag of litter!

Good manners demonstrate respect. Far from simply representing old-fashioned behavior, they show kindness and consideration toward others. Preschool children won't remember all of the dos and don'ts of social etiquette, but they will get the message that manners are important. That message helps build the foundation for good behavior.

1

Polite or Impolite?

Purpose

To help children learn the differences between polite and impolite behaviors

Materials Small table and chairs set up in the story corner, three dolls, paper or plastic drinking glasses, napkins, play cookies or another snack item

Procedure Discuss the definitions of the words *polite* and *impolite*, emphasizing the importance of being courteous to others and treating them as you would like to be treated. Tell the children that the dolls are having a snack together, and you want to see if the children can tell when the dolls are being polite or impolite.

Here is one way to conduct the exercise. Introduce the dolls: "These are my friends, Latisha, Mary, and Punnah." Then ask, "If Latisha says, 'Please pass the cookies,' is she being polite or impolite?" Explain that saying "please" is a polite way to ask for something.

Ask, "If Punnah is telling a story about his pet dog and his mouth is full of cookies, is he being polite or impolite?" Explain that everyone should swallow their food before speaking.

Ask, "If Mary would like more cookies and she says, 'I want more cookies,' is she being polite or impolite?" Explain that it is better to say, "May I please have more cookies?"

Ask, "If Punnah spills his milk on Latisha and he says, 'I'm sorry, that was an accident, and I will clean up the milk,' is he being polite or impolite?" Explain that Punnah is being polite, because saying "sorry," even when something was an accident, can help other people feel better. Also mention that he is being responsible for his mistake by offering to clean up.

Ask, "If Mary uses a napkin to wipe her mouth, is she being polite or impolite?" Explain that everyone should always use napkins, and not clothes, to wipe their mouths.

Ask, "If Latisha says, 'No, thank you,' when the teacher asks her if she would like more juice, is she being polite or impolite?" Explain that when people do not want something, they should say, "No, thank you."

Dramatize situations that have occurred in your classroom during snacktime.

Read   *I Show Respect!* by David Parker (2004), *I Accept You as You Are!* by David Parker (2004), and *I Care about Others!* by David Parker (2004)

2 Tea Party

Purpose

To help children practice good manners in a special setting

Materials

Toy tea set, manila drawing paper, napkins, snack, water or milk, real or artificial flowers, vase, newspaper or large sheets of colored tissue paper, masking tape, markers and crayons

Procedure

Plan an end-of-the-year tea party where children can practice their good manners. At all times, be sure to demonstrate good manners yourself, because modeling is one of the most powerful influences on children. Use the tea party as practice for the children to learn manners by using "Please," "Thank you," "Please pass the teapot," "Excuse me," and other pleasantries when appropriate. Invite parents to join in, and provide special tea party treats. Invite the children to bring a favorite doll or stuffed animal.

To prepare for the party, ask the children to make place settings by decorating sheets of manila paper. Help them arrange a centerpiece using flowers and a vase. Make party hats. Adorable hats can be made by laying two or three sheets of newspaper or colored tissue paper on top of a child's head. Rotate each piece so the corners are not lined up. Then tape the sheets snugly down over the outside around the child's head at eyebrow level. Now roll, fold, or otherwise pull up and adhere the corners of the paper in a variety of ways to style hats differently. Ask the children to remove their hats and decorate them.

Then let the party begin. Have everyone sit around the table. Allow children to pour from the teapot while they recite, "One, two, three. That's enough for me." The counting helps them pour without overfilling their cups. Encourage polite conversation and behavior.

Read *Miss Spider's Tea Party* by David Kirk (Scholastic 1994), *Suppose You Meet a Dinosaur: A First Book of Manners* by Judy Sierra (2012), and *Excuse Me! A Little Book of Manners* by Karen Katz (2002)

3

Sneeze Pictures

Purpose

To help children learn to consider other people when coughing or sneezing and to reduce communicable diseases

Materials   Construction paper, glue, markers or crayons, facial tissue

Procedure   Discuss with the children the importance of covering their mouths when they cough or sneeze. Explain that no one wants to give colds to others.

   Ask the children to draw a simple face on the construction paper and glue a facial tissue directly over the nose and mouth. The picture can be displayed in the classroom or at home and will serve as a great reminder.

Read   *Those Mean Nasty Dirty Downright Disgusting but . . . Invisible Germs* by Judith Anne Rice (1997)

4

Listening Skills

Purpose

To give children the experience of an atmosphere that encourages good listening

Materials Various

Procedure A strong connection exists between being a good listener and having respect for others. Listening to children shows them that we value them and care about what they have to say. Attentive listening is also fundamental to children's ability to internalize information. Use the following ideas to increase listening skills and enhance the children's enjoyment of listening:

- Tell a story while you and the children are under a blanket or parachute.

- Use different lighting, such as a flashlight, spotlight, or battery-operated candle while you tell a story.

- Paint a cozy living room scene on a refrigerator box. Center the scene on a painted fireplace. Cut out the area around the painted flames and place lighting (lamps or flashlights) behind them. Apply streaks of glue on the flames, and sprinkle with red and gold glitter. Hold story time around this hearth in the winter months.

- Buy a small microphone with a speaker. (Our program purchased a karaoke system with coupons through the Scholastic Book Club.) The microphone gets the children's attention, helps save your voice, can be used for making transition announcements, and is useful for other activities.

- Use props to complement story time to improve children's attentiveness. For example, use a teddy bear when reading a book about a bear, and use tiny, twinkling lights when you read about fireflies.

- Make a fake campfire for spring and summer programs. Add foil flames and a flashlight to the center of a circle of wooden blocks. Set up a tent in the room.
- Play recordings of sound effects.

5

Recycling Sort

Purpose

To familiarize children with recycling and keeping their surroundings clean

Materials   Empty, recyclable plastic, glass, and metal containers; newspapers; paper grocery bags; markers; work gloves

Procedure   Label each paper grocery bag with a picture identifying the type of recyclable material to be collected in that bag. Place all the recyclable items on a table, and allow the children to sort them into the correct bags.

On another day, encourage the children to wear work gloves and collect litter under close supervision, in their outdoor play area. Ask them to carefully help you identify and sort any recyclable items they may find.

6

Earth Care

Purpose

To become aware and respectful of the environment

Materials   Various

Procedure   Use these activities to help children create an environmentally friendly classroom:

- Recite the "Litterbug Poem":

  Litterbug, litterbug, that's not nice.
  Litterbug, litterbug, you better think twice.
  Litterbug, litterbug, don't you care?
  Litterbug, litterbug, let's be fair!

- Sing the following song to the tune of "London Bridge Is Falling Down":

  Look for litter and pick it up,
  Pick it up, pick it up.
  Look for litter and pick it up,
  Help our earth stay clean.

- Stress process, not product, in the classroom. Instead of having children paint on paper all the time, give them objects that they can paint and wash off to paint again. Examples of repaintable objects include pumpkins, seashells, rocks, dishes, and washable dolls.

- Paint walls and sidewalks outside with rollers, large brushes, and ice-cream buckets filled with water colored by a few drops of food coloring.

- Instead of buying new items, shop at garage sales, the Salvation Army, Goodwill stores, flea markets, secondhand shops, and junkyards for treasures that cost next to nothing. Make a point of telling children that buying these things secondhand is a form of recycling.

Suggestions   Keep recycling bins in the classroom for construction paper scraps, newspaper print, and other recyclables. The Environmental Education Toolkit for Early Childhood Family Education Programs can be downloaded free at www.rethinkrecycling.com/downloads/ecfe -tool-kit. Some of its information is specific to Minnesota residents, but a lot of the content is useful for everyone.

Read   *50 Simple Things You Can Do to Save the Earth* by John Javna, Sophie Javna, and Jesse Javna (2008), *The New 50 Simple Things Kids Can Do to Save the Earth* by Sophie Javna (2009), and *The Earth Book* by Todd Parr (2010).

7 Bird Feeders

Purpose

To help children develop empathy for nature

Materials Pinecones, peanut butter, birdseed, plastic knives, string

Procedure If you live in an area where the seasons change dramatically, talk about birds and explain that it's hard for them to find food in the winter. To help the birds, you are going to make bird feeders.

Have the children spread the peanut butter over a cone then roll it in a bowl of birdseed. You can make your own mix by combining nuts and seeds, such as sunflower seeds, millet, thistle seeds, and yellow corn. Hang the feeder on string where it's easy to view.

If anyone in your group of children has a peanut butter allergy, you can make bird feeders from recycled milk cartons instead. Cut openings on opposite sides of a clean carton, poke holes below the openings, and slip a dowel through the holes. Fill the bottom with your birdseed mix, and hang the feeder outside.

8

Using Sign Language

Purpose

To help children learn to communicate visually so they can increase their cooperation and understanding with all people

Materials   Commonly used signs appropriate for young children are illustrated in appendix B, page 145. The website www.lifeprint.com provides free self-study lessons, including an American Sign Language dictionary, videos, and a printable sign language alphabet chart.

Procedure   Sign language is an enjoyable and motivating way to help children stay focused. Sign language also makes communication possible for young toddlers who have not yet learned to speak and for children who do not speak the same language as the teacher. Sign language enhances communication for visual learners. Use signs along with your words, and you will be amazed by how quickly the children catch on.

Read   *My First 100 Words (Sign Language)* by Michiyo Nelson (2008)

Chapter 6 ✿ Self-Control

The greatest battle to be won is with ourselves.
—Earnie Larsen

Self-control is a prerequisite to respect. Children must develop their own control. Their good behavior does not necessarily mean that they have acquired self-control; a controlling adult may be responsible for it rather than a self-imposed restraint. Externally imposed control can become a problem if children feel out of control when the controller is not around. They may build resentment and anger toward the controlling person. Out of frustration, they may one day decide to take control and rebel.

I have found that one of the most effective ways to shape behavior is by letting specific children overhear me compliment them in a conversation with another child or adult. This indirect form of communication is very motivating to children, and you can actually see how touched they are when they hear what you are saying.

For example, Anne is working on her social skills and needs to gain confidence. During snacktime, I tell the classroom aide, within Anne's hearing, "Did you see Anne over at the writing center? She shared her marker with Luis! She is learning how to make friends at school." The aide then says something like, "Well, I saw Anne invite Tanya to play at the water table. She really does know how to make friends!"

Some children need extra help while they are developing self-control. Instead of relying only on speech, you can add a visual component, like American Sign Language, hand signals, or red and green flash cards to signal "yes" or "no" behaviors to children. This silent form of behavior shaping is less disruptive to the rest of the group and provides a gentle nudge to children who are still trying to master self-control.

1

Simon Says

Purpose

To help children learn to listen to and follow other people's directions

Materials   None

Procedure   Simon Says is a great game for self-control, listening skills, and motor planning. It's an oldie but a goodie! Explain to the children that they should only follow commands that begin with "Simon says." Instead of eliminating children who fail to follow the game correctly, reinforce the children who listen and follow the rule by praising their behavior.

2

The Great Predictor

To help children learn to predict the impact of their own and others' behavior

Materials A costume turban (or one made from wrapping a towel around the head) with a large feather plume

Procedure The children take turns being the Great Predictor; that is, they wear the turban and answer questions directed to them by the teacher. Each question begins with "Oh, Great Predictor . . . " followed by a question meant to get the children thinking about the consequences and rewards of their actions. Here are some sample questions:

- What happens if we are polite and friendly to everyone at school?
- What happens if we get angry and hit someone?
- What happens if we don't put our toys back where they belong?
- What do you do if someone calls you bad names?
- What happens if we share?
- What happens if we forget to put the caps on the markers?
- What could happen if we don't wash our hands before eating?
- What do you do if someone pushes you down?

Suggestion Invent questions that are relevant to issues in your own classroom.

3

Recycled Timers

Purpose

To help children practice patience and self-control; to help them learn that waiting can be fun; to give them concrete experiences of time; to introduce them to recycling

Materials   Two clean eight-ounce plastic pop bottles, colored sand, fine glitter for visual interest (a quarter cup equals about five minutes), two-hole button, clear tape, clock

Procedure   Pour the sand into one bottle. You can adjust the time by adding or removing some sand; I recommend no longer than five minutes. Place a two-hole button large enough to cover the top of the bottle's opening over its opening. Stack the second bottle upside down on top, and secure it with several layers of clear tape.

Use the timer at circle time to hold children's attention for five minutes of quiet time, in which they can look at books, deep breathe, do body stretches, or see who can be still for the whole five minutes.

4

Turn Taking

Purpose

To help preschoolers learn the very important social skill of taking turns

Materials   Various

Procedure   During circle time, pass out basic shapes cut from colored construction paper. Let each child choose one. Next, tell the children they are going to trade their shapes with a friend, and everybody should say, "Trade!" Demonstrate trading with a child. Sing this song to the tune of "Twinkle, Twinkle, Little Star."

Put your shape up in the air;
hold it high and keep it there.
Put your shape onto your back.
Now please place it on your lap.
Put your shape onto your nose.
Now please place it by your toes.

After singing, ask everyone to trade with a friend.

You can pass out a variety of seasonal or concept items for this activity: apples in the fall, paper snowflakes in winter, or faces depicting basic emotions. Practice sharing by passing out items to only half of the children, and when the song is over, ask them to share with a friend rather than trade.

This game makes sharing and trading easy. Once children have successfully shared and traded in a game, they are more likely to share during free play.

5

Potion Lotion

Purpose

To help children learn to control their body motions

Materials   Small plastic bottle of baby oil, glitter, tape, music

Procedure   Put the glitter inside the bottle of baby oil, and tape the bottle tightly shut to make the magical potion. Tell the children they are going to dance around the room, but they must try not to touch or bump into anyone else. To help them do that, they are going to rub an imaginary magical potion on their bodies. Demonstrate to them how to apply the potion by pretending to open up the bottle and rub the lotion on your arms, legs, head, shoulders, and feet. Pass the bottle around so that the children can do the same. Make sure they do not actually open the bottle.

While the music plays, encourage the children to move freely about the room without touching each other. If they do touch another child, ask them if they need more magic potion to help them control their movements.

6

Stop, Go, and Slow Necklace

Purpose

To help children guide their own behavior by giving them visual cues

Materials   Three sheets of red, green, and yellow rubber foam; hole punch; key ring; long string or necklace

Procedure   This prop is for the adults in charge. It is very useful for visual learners. Cut out three two-by-three-inch rectangles, one of each color. Punch a hole in the center top of each one, and put them on a metal key ring. Hang the key ring on a necklace or string around your neck. Explain to the children that red means "stop," green means "go," and yellow means "slow."

Make a game using the three rectangles and a variety of action commands, and later use the necklace to help shape positive behaviors without needing to say a word!

7

Penguins

Purpose

To help children develop self-control, turn taking, patience, and consideration for others

Materials　Construction paper, clear contact paper

Procedure　Cut out apple shapes, place them in a line on the floor, number them, and then cover them with clear contact paper. They hold up amazingly well. The numbers add a cognitive bonus.

　　Start out slowly; the children need a lot of physical help lining up and moving up the line one at a time. Have the youngest children stand at the front of the line to ensure more success. At circle time, before they wash their hands, ask the children to go and stand on an apple. Once they are in line, explain, "We are going to stand in line like penguins. We are going to take turns washing our hands. When someone goes to the sink, move to the next apple." Next, you can sing "I'm a Penguin." The numbered apple props provide visual cues, the flapping arms promote physical movement, the singing guides children with sound, and together these take the edge off the otherwise boring task of standing in line for fidgety preschoolers. When you break this task down to its simplest skills, children can learn, cooperate, and make transitions beautifully.

"I'm a Penguin" by Judith Anne Rice*

(*Sung to the tune of "Oh, My Darling Clementine"*)

I'm a penguin, I'm a penguin
and I'm standing in a line
I'm a penguin, I'm a penguin
and I'm doing just fine!

* *The children should hold their arms straight at their sides and flap them up and down like a penguin's wings.*

For a video demonstration, go to www.JudithAnneRice.com.

8

Choo-choo Game

Purpose

To help children practice cooperation and self-control

Materials   *Freight Train* by Donald Crews (1978); removable masking tape; three signs: red (stop), yellow (slow down), green (go)

Procedure   Use masking tape to create train tracks around the floor of the room. Read the story *Freight Train.* Assign roles from the book by asking, "Who would like to play . . . ?" Assign children to the green cattle car, purple boxcar, other cars, engine, caboose, and the three signs. Ask the children to form the train along the tracks by holding one another about the waist and chugging along the track. Instruct them to move past the green sign, slow down at the yellow one, and stop at the red sign. After a couple of trips around the track, change the locations of the signs.

9

My Day at School

Purpose

To help children develop self-awareness by monitoring their own behavior

Materials Copies of the My Day at School sheet (appendix A, page 138), one for each child; clipboard; pencil

Procedure Children who need extra help in reaching a behavioral goal, such as learning to share or not hitting others, can use the My Day at School sheet. Working with the child, decide on a goal. Discuss the goal with parents, and ask them to sign the sheet each day so you know they have been informed of their child's progress. The parents' involvement is crucial to supporting and holding the child accountable for attaining the goal.

The sheet should be placed on a clipboard with an attached pencil in a place accessible to the child. The child is responsible for placing a check mark in the smiling face or crossed-out smiling face column of the sheet, depending on behavior. At appropriate times (depending on the goal), you should ask the child to evaluate his actions and check off the proper box. At first the child may need close guidance, but eventually he will be able to evaluate his own behavior.

At the end of the day, discuss the results on the sheet with the child, and send the sheet home to be signed and returned to you the next day. The goal here is to help the child succeed in meeting his goals. If he is not succeeding, try another method in place of this activity.

Read *Without Spanking or Spoiling: A Practical Approach to Toddler and Preschool Guidance* by Elizabeth Crary (1993)

10

The Talking Wand

Purpose

To help children become better listeners and control the urge to interrupt others

Materials   Wand or toy microphone

Procedure   Discuss with the children that it is impolite to interrupt while someone else is talking. To help them remember this, only the person who has raised her hand and is holding the wand (or microphone) may talk. If only one person is speaking, everyone can hear and understand what is being said. Everyone can practice being a good listener.

Read   *I Am Responsible!* by David Parker (2004)

Chapter 7 ⚘ Friendship

Friendships divide our troubles and multiply our joys.
—Unknown

Friendships offer children companionship and fun. They provide opportunities to communicate, compromise, and create independence. Children's lives are enriched by the support and kindness they give and receive. Although their early childhood friendships are usually temporary ones and their friends are whomever the child happens to be playing with, it's nonetheless important for young children to learn how to make friends.

Because this subject interests them, you automatically have their attention whenever you talk about friendship. While you have their ears, teach them some basic rules about friends and friendship:

- Friends are kind to each other.

- Friends share their toys. When a conflict arises over a toy, you can encourage children to trade, share, or take turns, depending on the situation and the children's developmental age.

- Friends share their friends. Children may assert ownership over a playmate's friendship by saying, "She's my friend, not yours." Remind them that they can have many friends and that they need to share their friends with others.

- It's okay if someone doesn't want to play. Teach children that if someone doesn't want to play with them, that's okay—they can find another friend or something else to do. Learning to deal with rejection is an important skill.

Some friendship situations provide opportunities for children to learn more about their own feelings. For example, two kids playing together may say to a third who is trying to join their play, "You're not our friend; you can't play with us." What they may mean but don't know how to say is that they are having fun playing together right now and don't want a third person to join. Or they may not want to play because of something the other child has done. Help them learn to understand and say what they really mean.

To help children initiate friendly play, model "Let's" statements like "Let's share" or "Let's play house." These give children the language they need to make friendly overtures and join others in play. "Let's" statements can be followed by suggestions about play roles, for example, "You can be the mommy, and I'll be the daddy." You can suggest these roles by asking open-ended questions: "Who wants to be the driver? or the mommy? the doctor? the construction worker?"

Teach children how to notice and compliment each other's skills. It takes them awhile to learn how to give compliments. To help them learn, encourage them to assist others by assigning daily helping jobs like hand-washing assistant and coat helper. Then compliment their ability to perform their roles. You can also invite children to help others by putting their skills to use: "Sara, you're such a wonderful builder! Let's help Tomas build a zoo," and "Yasmina, can you show Tyler where the blocks belong?"

A circle-time game that asks children to think of something nice to say about another person provides good opportunities for children to practice giving compliments. To encourage this kind of reciprocal play, talk first to the children about turn taking, trading, and sharing. Help them learn to use the sentence "You can have it when I'm done." I first heard this from a child in my class years ago, and it has proven to be magic. A child who has something another child wants can use the sentence to hold on to the object a while longer, and the other child feels relief just knowing that he'll get his turn.

1

Hi and Bye Child

Purpose

To offer children opportunities to practice inclusive behavior and friendly manners

Materials None

Procedure Assign one child each day to stand at the door and be the "Hi and Bye child." That child greets new arrivals and makes a point of saying good-bye when anyone leaves.

2 Friendship Fruit Soup

Purpose

To help children practice cooperation and to share healthy food with friends

Materials Large bowl, ladle, cutting board, knife, manual can opener, paper cups, soup spoons, fresh or canned fruits, large can or bottle of cherry juice

Procedure Ask the children to bring to school their favorite fresh or canned fruits to share with their friends. Explain that some cultures serve a hot or cold fruit soup before their main course. Berries, cherries, and plums are the favored contents for a fruit soup. Tell the children that they will make their own version of fruit soup.

Before preparing it, make sure the children have thoroughly washed their hands. Then help them clean and carefully cut up their fresh fruits. Add canned fruits to the bowl, along with enough cherry juice to ensure a soupy consistency. Stir, serve in the paper cups, and enjoy.

3

Shake Shake Shake

Purpose

To help children form friendships

Materials   None

Procedure   Ask the children to form two circles, one inside the other. The children in one ring should be facing those in the other. As they sing "Shake Shake Shake," the children shake hands with those they face. After each verse, the inner circle rotates to the left so each child has a new shaking partner.

"Shake Shake Shake" by Judith Anne Rice

(*to the tune of "London Bridge Is Falling Down" or "Here We Go Round the Mulberry Bush"*)

Shake your hand with someone new [*shake hands*],
How do you do?
How are you?
Shake your hand with someone new,
Who are you?

Read   *How Do Dinosaurs Play with Their Friends?* by Jane Yolen (2006) and *Smiling* by Gwenyth Swain (1999)

4 Firefly Game

Purpose

To help children form friendships and identify their classmates

Materials   Flashlight

Procedure   Form a circle and turn down the room lights. Appoint one child as the firefly, who holds the flashlight, shines it about, and stops the beam on another child while reciting,

Firefly, firefly, oh so bright!
Firefly, firefly, shines at night.
I see [*another child's name*].

The child named now receives the flashlight and becomes the next firefly.

Suggestion   Add atmosphere to the activity by stringing tiny white or yellow blinking holiday lights around the room.

Read   *The Very Lonely Firefly* by Eric Carle (1995)

5

Best Smile

To help children develop body awareness and a positive attitude; to practice a sure way to welcome friendship

Materials   Crayons; blank face picture (appendix A, page 136), one for each child; several mirrors

Procedure   Discuss smiling with the children. Explain that smiling is a way to show others that they like them and that they like themselves. Ask the children to practice smiling in front of a mirror. Then ask each child to demonstrate his *best* smile to the class. Now hand out a copy of the face pictures to all the children and have them draw their best smiles.

Read   *Smiling* by Gwenyth Swain (1999)

6

Friendship Map

Purpose

To help children develop friendships, creativity, and self-esteem

Materials   Road map, very large sheet of butcher's paper, crayons or markers, toy cars

Procedure   Have the children sit around the paper. Show them a real map and discuss how it is used. Ask them to draw a house on the paper next to where they are sitting.

Allow one child at a time to draw lines representing a road or street or highway leading from her house to the house of a friend. Label each child's road, for example, "Andre's Drive" or "Hannah's Highway." When all the children have had a turn, give them toy cars to use on the mapped roads for dramatic play.

7

Hug a Bug

Purpose

To encourage children's friendships and help children learn to touch friends in appropriate ways

Materials   Tape or CD player; music

Procedure   Play fun dance music. When the music stops, the children must find one or several others to gently hug until the music resumes. Then they can dance again.

Read   *Hug* by Jez Alborough (2000)

8

Fishing for Friends

Purpose

To help children identify classmates with whom they can develop friendships. Really fun!

Materials   Photos of individual classmates, smooth-edged metal juice lids, fishing poles, magnets

Procedure   Before class, glue the children's photos onto the metal lids. Attach the magnets to the fishing poles. Ask the children to sit in a circle, and scatter the juice lids in the center of the circle. Give one child a fishing pole, and instruct her to fish for a classmate by dangling her line over the pile of lids. Once she has caught a friend, that child gets the pole and takes her turn fishing. The juice lid is returned to the center, and the pole is passed from child to child according to the catch.

Once children understand the game, you can hand out several poles to be used simultaneously.

9

Let's Play

Purpose

To give children language for joining others in play

Singing "Let's Play!" reinforces the language children need for joining others in play. Sing it during group time. Model the song first, and then ask individual children to think of something they like to do with friends. Then have them fill in the blank in the third verse with their own choice of activity.

Materials   Song "Let's Play!"

Procedure   Teach the song "Let's Play":

"Let's Play" by Judith Anne Rice
(*sung to the tune of "Me and My Teddy Bear"*)

Me and my friends have fun,
Let's play puppets, let's go run.

Me and my friends at school,
Let's play, let's play all day.

Me and my friends have fun,
Let's [*insert activity*], let's go run.

Me and my friends at school,
Let's play, let's play all day.

Chapter 8   Conflict Resolution

The only way to settle a disagreement is on the basis of what's right—not who's right.
—Apples of Gold

Children need to learn that a certain amount of conflict is natural. Our job as teachers and caregivers is to provide them with experiences and help them develop skills to handle conflict appropriately. Once they can do that, they will see that conflict is a challenging *part* of life but doesn't have to become a *way* of life. When children do not learn how to deal with conflicts and painful feelings peacefully, and when educators and parents do not know how to address hurtful behaviors effectively, what begins as developmentally appropriate behavior at two can become an engrained pattern that eventually is labeled *bullying*. Betsy Evans (2012, 56), a conflict resolution and bullying specialist for HighScope, describes the problem succinctly: "A hurtful preschool behavior can become a pattern of bullying only when it is *repeated, intense, and targeted.*" It's our job to prevent that from happening, because childhood bullying can lead to a wide range of behavioral and health problems.

Our aim is to help children learn to solve their own conflicts effectively and to prevent "repeated, intense, and targeted" behaviors from occurring among the children we care for. This means helping children address problems from the very small to the very big. We mustn't focus solely on the child who is the aggressor: the child who is being picked on must also learn how to respond to the other child's behavior constructively.

I've found that several techniques are key to helping children learn how to resolve conflicts effectively:

- Use "I" messages instead of "You" messages—"You" messages convey accusation.
- Make eye contact during conversation, culture permitting.
- Find their own solutions to problems.
- Find appropriate ways to express anger.
- Name and articulate feelings.

When low-level conflicts arise, ask the children to talk directly to one another rather than through you. This builds their self-confidence and gives them real practice solving problems. Initially, they may need a lot of help, but with practice they can learn to exchange views with their peers without your assistance.

More commonly, children are denied the opportunity to learn problem-solving skills because the adults in their lives don't believe young children can solve their own conflicts. In fact, children are naturally forgiving and feel empowered when they solve conflicts themselves.

I teach the children in my classes these three steps, which have proven very effective in conflict resolution:

1. Look at the other child and state the child's name: "Sarah" [*ensures listening*].

2. Give an "I" message: "I feel sad when you don't share" [*informs*].

3. Tell the other child what you want: "Let's share" [*offers solution*].

When you discuss possible solutions with children, ask them how a particular solution makes them feel. Ask them how they think the solution might make the other person feel. When you do this, you teach them that solutions should be fair and take other people's feelings into consideration.

Sometimes conflicts do not involve another person, such as when a child is upset because he can't find a place to sit down during lunch, even though there's an empty chair nearby. Instead of telling the child where to sit, ask him questions that help him locate the open chair and choose to join the other children.

When you emphasize conflict too much, you run the risk that children will think it's a bigger part of life than it has to be; they may expect and create conflict where it doesn't exist. In the classroom, try to strike a balance that favors positive relationships. Treat conflicts as opportunities for the children to think about how to solve them.

Restitution is a concept you can introduce to preschoolers to help them think about what they can say or do to make up for mistakes or accidents before those escalate into conflicts. Emphasize the importance of resolving problems fairly. Children's restitution can take the form of saying things like, "I'm sorry—can I help you rebuild with the blocks I knocked down?" or "Are you okay?" or "How can I help?" and "Next time I will use words when I get mad."

If they spill, give them the tools they need to clean up their mess. If they tear a page out of a book, give them the tape they need to repair it. You may need to redo their repairs, but you have helped them learn how to make amends. These lessons will serve them their entire lives. Instead of always providing the answers for the children, you might say one of the following:

- "It looks like we don't have a shovel for everybody. Does anybody have an idea about what we could do?"

- "It looks like you are feeling angry about George knocking down your castle. Is there something you could say to him?"

- "Are you feeling sad? May I give you a hug or may I read a story to you?"

- "Our room is messy. Does anybody have any good ideas about how we can get it cleaned up?"

- "Ashley hit Mario. The rule is no hitting. This is a problem. What should Ashley do? What should Mario do?"

The Road to Bullying

Sometimes, though, the gentle, reciprocal techniques that resolve most early childhood conflicts are not enough. You may need a bigger toolbox to prevent children's hurtful behaviors if they are becoming, in Evans's words, "repeated, intense, and targeted."

Evans (2012, 58) offers six strategies to help adults prevent bullying among young children:

1. Understand the difference between a pattern of bullying and predictable preschool behaviors.

2. Avoid general directives such as "Let's all be friends" and "Be nice."

3. Problem solve when there are conflicts or hurtful comments.

4. Set limits on any intimidating behaviors, and follow up with positive interactions.

5. Recognize hurtful behaviors that are intense and repeated as a possible red flag that children need more attention to the reasons behind their behaviors and provide consistent problem-solving guidance as they learn to express their feelings more constructively.

6. Eliminate bullying by adults: examine adult behaviors for the use of yelling, shaming, threatening, and/or punishing in interactions with young children.

Although bullying behavior by preschool children is unlikely to occur, it definitely appears in some classrooms once children become kindergartners and primary school students. I believe that *The Kindness Curriculum*, lovingly implemented, strengthens young children and prepares them to hold their own when confronted by powerfully hurtful behaviors of other children. I believe that *The Kindness Curriculum* also helps children learn when they should seek adult help in conflicts.

A valuable lesson of research by Betsy Evans, Wendy Craig, Anita Remig, and others who study bullying and behavioral modification is the importance of providing five positive interactions for every limit-setting one. This one-to-five ratio is evidence based. For detailed discussions of it, see Evans (2012) and Remig (2009).

1

Helping Hands

Purpose

To teach children that hands are for helping

Materials   Helping hands pledge reproducible (appendix A, page 139); markers or crayons

Procedure   Talk with the children, explaining that hands are for helping, not for hurting. Talk about all of the good things that hands do for us and for others. Ask the children to trace their hands and sign the pledge to use their hands for helping. Display the pledges, and use them to reinforce helpers and remind hitters!

Read   *Hands Are Not for Hitting* by Martine Agassi (2009)

2

What Can We Do?

Purpose

To familiarize children with problem-solving techniques

Materials   Photos of the children sharing, trading, waiting, taking turns, calming, or shaking hands; square box about six by six inches, taped closed; clear contact paper; scissors; glue

Procedure   Mount one photo on each side on the cube, and cover with clear contact paper. Initially, use the cube to familiarize the children with the six possible actions on the sides of the box. When a conflict arises, roll the cube and talk about the solution that appears on top of the box. If the suggestion does not apply or the child wants to try something else, roll the box again.

3

My Turn, Your Turn

Purpose

To help children practice taking turns and patience

Materials Collection of small toys

Procedure Explain to the children that learning to take turns is one of their jobs. Pair them off, seated face-to-face, and give one child in the pair a toy. Instruct her to hold it and say, "My turn." After five seconds, tell her to give the toy to her partner and say, "Your turn." The partner then accepts the toy, says, "My turn," and five seconds later is told to return the toy to the first child, saying, "Your turn." Repeat.

Note: This is a painless way for children to practice an important social skill. The last few times they take turns, lengthen the waiting time to ten seconds. Discuss with them how it feels to wait. Some kids may find that ten seconds is a long time to wait. Ask them to think of things they can do while they are sitting and waiting. Tell them that waiting calmly is called *patience* and that learning to be patient will help them be happy.

4

Problem-Solving Table

Purpose

To help children learn to sit down together and peacefully find solutions to conflicts

Materials

Table-size cardboard box, tape, serrated knife, newspapers, tempera paint, paintbrushes, copies of six feeling faces (appendix A, page 137), crayons

Procedure

Before class, tape the opening of the box shut. Cut out the sides, leaving enough cardboard to serve as support or legs. Explain to the children that they are making a problem-solving table where they can sit down with other children to talk about solving problems. Ask the children to create some rules to be followed at the table. Here are some examples:

- Be a good listener.

- Be honest.

- Think of ways to solve the problem.

Participating in creating the table and rules increases children's ability to learn from using the table. Lay out newspapers to protect the floor, and ask the class to paint the table.

Be sure to place the table in an area that is as quiet and private as possible. Put copies of the six feelings faces sheet on the table with crayons so the children can use it to help identify their feelings. When a conflict arises that cannot easily be resolved, bring the children to the table. Mediate their discussion, reminding them if necessary of the rules they created. Help them decide for themselves the best solution. If you are not up to making a problem-solving table, just designate a spot in the classroom for sitting down and solving conflicts.

Suggestion   Familiarize children with simple methods to help them solve their problems, such as sharing, humor, taking turns, chance (flipping a coin), and compromising.

Read   *Here Comes the Cat* by Frank Asch (1989), a delightful tale with a very surprising ending

5

Kid Cards

Purpose

To provide children with tools for solving problems, handling emotions, and resolving conflicts appropriately

Materials   Kid Cards (appendix A, pages 140–43)

Procedure   Divide the Kid Cards into groups for dealing with different situations. Keep the cards available at all times, and use them as often as possible to familiarize children with ways to solve conflicts and deal effectively with their feelings. Choose the cards appropriate to the situation, and go through each one with the children, asking, "Do you think this might work?" Let them decide which solution would work best. You can create your own cards to address recurring situations unique to your classroom and for children with special interests or needs.

I'm Feeling Mad

- I can take a time out.
- I can tear paper.
- I can cry awhile.
- I can get a tissue.
- I can pound drums.
- I can stomp my feet.
- I can break sticks.
- I can roll around.
- I can jump up and down.

I Have a Problem to Solve

- I can share.
- I can trade.
- I can take turns.
- I can flip a coin.
- I can talk about my feelings.
- I can wait.
- I can stop and think.

I Need to Calm Down

- I can take a deep breath.
- I can count.
- I can breathe with a tummy toy.
- I can blow bubbles.
- I can hug a stuffed toy.
- I can look at a book.
- I can rock a baby doll.
- I can stretch.

6

Turtle Puppets and Story

Purpose

To help children discover the "tuck and think" method of resolving conflicts

Materials   *Tucker Turtle Takes Time to Talk and Think*, a story available for free from the Center on the Social and Emotional Foundations for Early Learning website: http://csefel.vanderbilt.edu/resources/strategies .html; nine-inch paper plates; stapler; markers

Procedure   The Turtle Technique is a tool that young children can use to deal with angry feelings. It was developed by Teaching Tools for Young Children with Challenging Behavior. Through a scripted story available online, children learn to

1.   recognize their feelings,

2.   think "stop,"

3.   tuck inside their "shells" and take three deep breaths, and

4.   come out when they are calm and can think of a solution.

Read *Tucker Turtle Takes Time to Talk and Think* to the children and teach the Turtle Technique. Ask them to color their turtle shells. Staple two paper plates together, leaving an opening so children can slide their hands (the turtle's head) through the shell. Use washable marker to draw eyes on the hand that serves as the turtle's head. The children can practice the turtle method with their puppets and then with themselves.

Suggestion   Have the children perform their own turtle puppet plays.

7

The Stop Song

Purpose

To help children learn to assert themselves and teach them that hitting is unacceptable

Materials Song "Stop!"

Procedure Use the suggested moves to add emphasis while the children sing this song—they love it! The tune is demonstrated on www.JudithAnneRice.com

"Stop!" by Judith Anne Rice

(Visit www.JudithAnneRice.com to hear the tune to "Stop!")

Everybody say STOP!
'Cause hitting is bad [*use American Sign Language
    sign for* stop].
It makes me mad [*make a mad face*].
I feel real sad [*make a sad face*],
Say STOP! [*use sign for* stop]
We can talk it out,
No need to shout,
Be coooooooooooooool [*spread arms and hands apart
    and breathe deeply*].

Everybody say HELP! [*make the ASL sign for* help]
Say *no* to mean,
Don't be a jelly bean,
Tell what you've seen,
Say HELP! [*use sign for* help]
We can talk it out,
No need to shout,
Be coooooooooooooool [*spread arms and hands apart
    and breathe deeply*].

8

Mr. Peepers's Chants

Purpose

To teach replacement strategies using positive affirmations

Materials   Puppet (I use a ring puppet whom I call Mr. Peepers)

Procedure   Introduce your puppet to the children, and have it ask, "What can you do when you get mad?" The puppet then suggests, "I use words when I get mad." Clap and chant each phrase of the answers.

Another day, the puppet can ask, "What can you do when you have to wait?" Ask the children for answers, and then have the puppet suggest, "I'll find something else to do." Use the children's suggestions too. Another time, the puppet can ask, "What can you do if you get too excited?" Follow the preceding steps. You'll be surprised by how simple and effective these chants can be.

For a child who is not ready to share:

You can have it when I'm done,
You can have it when I'm done,
You can have it when I'm done.

For a child who hits:

I use words when I get mad,
I use words when I get mad,
I use words when I get mad.

For a child who doesn't want to wait for a turn:

I'll find something else to do,
I'll find something else to do,
I'll find something else to do.

For a child who is anxious:

I can calm my body down,
I can calm my body down,
I can calm my body down.

Suggestion   For a video demonstration, go to www.JudithAnneRice.com.

9

Learning to Ask for Help

Purpose

To teach children to ask for help when someone is getting hurt

Materials   None

Procedure   It is really important for young children to learn that it's okay to ask for help. Role playing allows children to practice the language they need to use when they're seeking help. In a group of children, practice asking for help. Select a child, and present him with an example of a situation in which he may need help. For instance, ask the following:

- "What should you do if someone hits you?"

- "What should you do if someone hits someone else?"

- "What should you do if someone throws sand at you?"

- "What should you do if someone pushes you down the slide?"

When a child chooses to ask for help, reinforce his decision. Say, "Thanks for asking for help!" When a child hesitates, guide him to the correct response, which is to ask for help. Remember to reinforce his choice. You don't have to query every child in the group; what's important is to let everyone know that it's important to feel okay about asking for help when someone is being hurt. Emphasize that hurting anyone is always against the rules.

Chapter 9   Visualization

The happiness of your life depends on the quality of your thoughts.
—*Apples of Gold*

Visualization combines relaxation, imaging, audio recordings, and guided imagery to help quiet the mind and aid concentration. It's an effective tool for improving children's behavior, boosting their learning skills, and fostering creativity.

A good example of how visualization works comes from one of the parents in the Early Childhood Family Education program where I teach. Sheryl often discussed her fears and feelings with me about being an "upset, out-of-control mom" and her frustration at her son Tyler's oppositional behavior. Because other techniques I had suggested had not helped, I asked Sheryl if she and Tyler would be willing to listen to two recordings that I could prepare for them. She agreed.

The first part of Sheryl's tape contained relaxation and deep breathing exercises and the second part positive messages about Sheryl being a calm, peaceful, loving mom. On Tyler's tape, I recorded messages about being a good listener, helper, and playmate.

A month later, Sheryl wrote me a letter describing the results: "I ask questions instead of screaming 'Do it now!' I feel in control of my life now. . . . I don't see things as doomed, I have a positive outlook and love my son, and I even feel he loves me again." The messages in her tape helped Sheryl form a new, positive picture of herself. Her behavior began to match her new image, just as it had matched her earlier self-image as an upset, out-of-control mom. Tyler, she said, had become more cooperative and a much better listener.

Visualization techniques can also be used in school to calm children, improve their behavior, reinforce learning, help create smooth transitions, and stimulate creativity. I use visualization at the end of each day for the five-year-olds enrolled in my learning readiness class. During our last ten minutes together, I ask the children to position themselves comfortably on the floor and close their eyes. I turn down the lights and play a soft lullaby in the background. We begin with deep breathing to calm our bodies, quiet our minds, and create a sense of peace. Then I use guided imagery; that is, I tell them a story that guides their imaginations to create pictures to help them reach an objective.

Visualizing helps children develop positive self-images, see their goals clearly, and focus on them. Visualization can be learned. The activities in this chapter help children learn the technique in a fun and effective way.

1

Imaging

Purpose

To help children learn how to visualize

Materials   None

Procedure   Use one of the calming activities from chapter 1, "Creating Calm." Then ask the children to close their eyes and see a picture of the common object you will describe in detail but not name. (The script below provides an example of this.) When you are finished describing it, the children will open their eyes and tell you what object they saw. Some children will have difficulty at first seeing pictures with their eyes closed; others will not. Talking to them like this can help them learn to visualize:

"Can you see things when you dream? What do you see? Can you hear or feel or taste or smell anything? When we dream, we are asleep and our eyes are closed. Today we are going to visualize; that is, we are going to try to see pictures with our eyes closed while we are awake!

"Let's play a game. I will describe or tell you about something. Try to see a picture of it while your eyes are closed. When I tell you to open your eyes, you can guess what it is that I described.

"I see something round and very, very bright. I feel warm rays of light coming from it. The light is golden and white. The rays from it make trees, flowers, and plants grow. It is very high up in the sky, and far, far away. A fluffy white cloud just floated past it. Open your eyes and raise your hand if you think you know what I was describing."

Read   *Bubble Riding: A Relaxation Story* by Lori Lite (2008)

2 Goal Pictures

Purpose

To help children create pictures that illustrate and motivate them to accomplish a goal

Materials   Tagboard, magazines, scissors, glue

Procedure   Ask each child to select, if need be with your help, an appropriate goal. Then help children choose pictures from magazines that symbolize that goal. Have them cut out the pictures and paste them onto tagboard squares to create collages. The collages should be displayed in a place where they can serve as reminders, motivators, and visual cheerleaders.

This activity can be used to enhance learning as well as to create or redirect behavior. Here are some examples:

- *Enhancing learning.* To help a child learn to identify colors, make a goal board of objects that are all one color. After the child can identify that color in her surroundings, she is ready to create a new goal board using another color.

- *Creating behavior.* If a child is shy and withdrawn but wants to learn how to make friends, cut out pictures of smiling faces, children playing together, and a favorite happy photograph of the child. Paste the pictures onto the tagboard. The child can display the board at home or keep it at school. Observing the collage can instill a more confident, friendly picture in the child, thus improving his self-concept and interactions with others.

- *Redirecting behavior.* If a child is having a problem with hitting, you and she can cut out pictures of hands helping, cooking, painting, holding, and performing other constructive acts. Discuss all the good things that hands can do. The resulting collage should be displayed prominently. If the child does hit and is taking a break or being disciplined in some other way, give her the collage to look at, and remind her of what hands are for.

Note: I have a friend who lost sixty pounds. One of her most effective motivating influences was a collage of healthy women who resembled her, which she mounted in front of her treadmill. She re-created her image of herself and made that image a reality.

3

Audio Recordings

Purpose

To reinforce children's positive behavior and improve their self-concepts

Materials   Written script, portable recorder, or cell phone

Procedure   Obtain the permission and cooperation of children's parents or guardians before making individual audio recordings for children. With the parents, decide what the children's goal(s) should be. Parents may choose to make the audio recording themselves, using either your script or one they have written.

Begin the audio recording by using messages that relax the child. Then create a story that sends positive messages and supports the goal. Make sure your voice is clear, calm, and slow. Read in a soothing tone, stretching out important words and pausing between sentences and after deep breaths. Avoid a monotonous tone; add expression to your voice to make the narrative interesting.

The audio recording is most effective when children listen to it just before bedtime. Its length depends on the attention span of the child but is typically about four minutes.

This is the script that I created for Tyler, Sheryl's son. The goal Sheryl and I agreed on was to improve Tyler's listening and cooperation. His tape runs about three and a half minutes and starts and ends with a music box playing a lullaby.

Tyler's Audio Recording

[*lullaby music*]

Time to go to sleep, Tyler.
Close your eyes.
Pretend you are floating on a magic carpet.
Slowly . . . slowly . . . next to the clouds.
Softly . . . gently . . . close your eyes.
Take a deep breath . . . breathe in . . . now, breathe out.

Slowly . . . relax . . .

Now you are starting to dream.

Someone is talking to you.

Could it be a genie from a magic land?

You can hear his voice clearly because you are a *very good* listener.

Say to yourself, "I am a very good listener.

My mom only needs to ask me one time because I can hear her with my ears.

I am a *good* listener."

The genie says, "Come to the palace and visit a princess, her tiger, and the prince."

Because you are a good listener, you can hear the genie.

Together, you fly on the carpet and land in the middle of the palace.

The palace is beautiful: plants and colorful flowers are everywhere.

The prince and princess come to greet you.

Then everyone plays happily together,

Sharing toys, cooperating, and when it's time to clean up, you are the very best helper of all.

Then you start to walk outside of the garden.

You see something very interesting.

The princess says, "Stop!"

Because you are such a good listener, the princess needs to tell you *only* one time.

She explains that everyone must stay within the palace walls.

That's the rule when you are visiting the palace.

Oops, time to go home.

You say "Good-bye."

The princess thanks you for being such a good listener, playmate, and helper.

Tyler *is* a good listener.

When Mom and Dad ask you to do something, you do it right away.

They only need to ask one time.

You are such a good playmate to Candy [*Tyler's baby sister*].

And when it's time to clean up, you are a wonderful helper.

Good night, Tyler.

You will have a good day tomorrow.

[*lullaby music*]

Note: Recall that Tyler's mother told me this tape was very effective when used faithfully.

Thinking Hats

Purpose

To stimulate children's thoughts, awareness, and imaginations by using a whimsical prop

There are many ways that preschoolers can make a hat, but my favorite is one made from a recycled paper grocery bag.

Materials Paper bags; one-inch elastic, approximately twenty inches per hat; crayons; markers; glue; feathers; art scraps

Procedure Children practice thinking while they wear their hats during think time. Explain to the class that thinking is one of the most important things they can do and that they'll put on their hats when you ask them to ponder things.

First, measure and cut a length of one-inch-wide elastic around the child's head, and staple the ends together. Place the paper bag upside down on the child's head. Encircle the elastic around the bag and the child's forehead. Roll up the edge of the bag to form a brim. The children can decorate the hats any way they want.

Read *Oh, the Thinks You Can Think!* by Dr. Seuss (1975) and *Oodles of Doodles* by Nikalas Catlow (2009)

5

Worry Objects

Purpose

To help children learn to take breaks from stress and worry in their lives

Materials Construction paper, markers

Procedure Precut butterflies for younger children (older children can cut out the butterflies themselves), and ask them to decorate them. Write their names on the butterflies so they can be reused (finding their butterflies is a fun way to increase children's literacy). Pass out the butterflies, and then ask the children to think of something they are worried, feel sad, or are afraid about. Next, ask them to whisper their worries to their butterfly. After a few moments of silence, quietly collect their butterflies (along with their worries), and tell them to let those feelings fly away for a while because they have so many fun things to do.

Read *Walter Was Worried* by Laura Vaccaro Seeger (2005), *Wemberly Worried* by Kevin Henkes (2000), *Counting Sheep* by Julie Glass (2000)

6

Practical Visualizations

Purpose

To help children incorporate visualization into everyday situations

Materials   None

Procedure   Here are some examples of how you can use visualization with children:

- You're taking the children on a field trip to a museum. Before you go, during quiet group time, ask the children to close their eyes and relax while you describe in detail what will happen on the trip. This simple exercise prepares the children psychologically. You will see an increase in their level of cooperation and overall enjoyment of the experience.

- Use the same simple visualization day after day. It's a great way to quickly calm and de-stress children. Once they have become quiet, tell them a story about resting on a cloud that passes through a rainbow and lands on a giant floating lily pad pulled by a team of butterflies. Over time, retelling this story will immediately relax and focus them.

- Individual visualizations are great for children who are working on specific behaviors or skills. Tell the story while the child is in a relaxed state, which makes her more receptive to the behavior or skill you are trying to encourage. For example, if you have a child who refuses to talk, once she is relaxed, then you can tell her a story about going to school and talking to the teacher, the other children, making friends—even singing! Once she can *imagine* herself talking, she will find it easier to make talking a reality.

Chapter 10  Parent and Child
Home Sweet Homework

Parents are the most powerful force in a child's life. The Parent and Child Home Sweet Homework sheets are designed to inform them of what their children are learning and to invite them to participate in their children's education. Encouraging parent participation at the very beginning of the educational process helps ensure parents' continued involvement in the schools, their communities, and most important, their children's lives.

The following pages include one sheet for each of the nine chapters in this book. The sheets should be copied and sent home with the child. After parents complete the assignment with their child, they sign and return it.

There is also a sheet called Television Literacy for Preschoolers that can be sent home with the children but does not need to be signed or returned by parents. The main purpose of this sheet is to inform parents of the American Academy of Pediatrics' recommendations regarding television viewing time for young children. The sheet also encourages parents to evaluate the content of the child's viewing.

After all the homework assignments are complete, each child can design a cover and staple it to the sheets, making a keepsake. The booklet will also serve as a reminder of some of life's most important lessons. Feel free to use the letter on the next page to communicate with the families.

Dear Parent or Guardian,

This is a worksheet for you and your child to complete together. We want you to know what we are learning about, and we invite you to participate.

With your child, please complete the assignment, sign it, and return it. Your child will make a book out of all the worksheets once they are completed.

Thank you!

_____

Teacher or caregiver's signature

Creating Calm

When children feel calm, they are more likely to make positive choices and will feel genuinely good about themselves. Taking a few minutes out of your day to calm down with your child is well worth it. Please complete the assignment, sign, and return.

Assignment

Circle the things that you already do, or are willing to try to do, together.

- "Freshersize." Combine fresh air and exercise in outdoor play with your child.

- Slowly count to ten when someone feels stressed.

- Breathe deeply five times.

- Whisper while you read a story to your child.

- Make up a secret handshake or silly dance that signals "I love you."

- Bend, stretch, and reach for the stars ten times.

- Splash your face with cool water to feel refreshed.

- Create a ritual like a tea party to connect with your child and talk about the day.

- Gaze at the night sky before going to bed. Pick out a star and make a wish.

- Turn off all electronic media at least one hour before your child's bedtime.

- Talk about good and bad feelings without judging. Say, "Tell me more."

Please sign:

_____

Parent's signature

_____

Child's signature

2

Love

A child's understanding of love can be built on healthy adult relationships he or she observes. Please complete the assignment, sign, and return.

Together with your child, commit an act of kindness by helping someone else. In the space provided, write down what you did.

Please sign: _____

Parent's signature

_____

Child's signature

3

Feelings and Empathy

When we talk about our feelings, it helps us understand each other. Please complete the assignment, sign, and return.

List your and your child's responses to what makes you feel:

HAPPY

    You:

    Your child:

SAD

    You:

    Your child:

ANGRY

    You:

    Your child:

EXCITED

    You:

    Your child:

Please sign: _____

Parent's signature

_____

Child's signature

4

Gentleness

Being gentle is a way to show we love each other. Please complete the assignment, sign, and return.

Assignment   Agree to hug each other every day.

Please sign: _____

Parent's signature

_____

Child's signature

5

Respect

It is important to respect ourselves, our parents, and the environment. Please complete the assignment, sign, and return.

Assignment   Write down a good way to show respect for:

1. Yourself

2. Your parents

3. The environment

Please sign: _____

Parent's signature

_____

Child's signature

6

Self-Control

Everybody feels angry sometimes. What we do with our angry feelings is very important. Please complete the assignment, sign, and return.

Assignment
Together with your child, circle the things we can do when we're angry, and cross out the things we shouldn't do when we're angry.

Talk about how you feel   Hit someone

Count to ten   Breathe deeply

Go to another room   Throw things

Take a bath   Call someone names

Please sign:
_____
Parent's signature

_____
Child's signature

7

Friendship

Friends care and share. Friends help and listen to each other. They share toys, take turns, and have fun together. Please complete the assignment, sign, and return.

Assignment   Ask your child for the names of his or her friends at school, and write them here.

Practice sharing. Write about something you shared.

Please sign: _____

Parent's signature

_____

Child's signature

8

Conflict Resolution

If we learn at an early age that conflicts can be resolved, then we will be more prepared to cope with our problems as adults. Every home should have a special place where the family can sit down together and think of ways to solve problems. There, everyone must agree to be a good listener, to be honest, and to try to cooperate. Please complete the assignment, sign, and return.

Assignment

Choose a problem-solving place in your home. Write down where it is.

Please sign:

_____

Parent's signature

_____

Child's signature

9

Visualization

When we close our eyes and make pictures in our minds, we are visualizing. Visualizing can help us learn and be creative. Please complete the assignment, sign, and return.

Assignment

Ask your child to get into a comfortable position, relax, and close his or her eyes. Slowly, clearly, and calmly read the following script to your child.

Breathe in. (Pause) Breathe out. (Pause) Breathe in. (Pause) Breathe out. (Pause) Relax. (Pause)

It's a very sunny, peaceful day. Let's go for a walk to a park. The park has green grass. Look at the colorful flowers. Listen to the birds singing. There are a lot of tall trees. The sky is blue and the sun is bright. There is even a pond with a family of ducks swimming in it.

Now you run, play, laugh, and enjoy breathing the fresh air and being outside. (Pause) Time to go home. But we'll come back another day.

Your child can slowly open his or her eyes now. Ask your child to draw a picture of the park on the back of this worksheet.

Please sign: _____

Parent's signature

_____

Child's signature

10 Television Literacy for Preschoolers

Dear parents,

We would like you to know what the American Academy of Pediatrics recommends about your child's television viewing time. Here is their statement:

> The first two years of your child's life are especially important in the growth and development of her brain. During this time, children need positive interaction with other children and adults. This is especially true at younger ages, when learning to talk and play with others is so important.
>
> Until more research is done about the effects of screen time on very young children, the American Academy of Pediatrics strongly discourages television viewing for children ages two years old or younger, and encourages interactive play.
>
> For older children, the Academy advises no more than one to two hours per day of educational, nonviolent programs, which should be supervised by parents or other responsible adults in the home.

Teach preschool children to recognize and choose nonviolent TV programs. List the names of TV programs your child watches. Together, circle the appropriate face depending on the value of the program content. Help children understand what violence means by explaining that it is someone getting hurt.

You do not need to return this sheet, but please continue to monitor your child's screen time, including television, computers, and video games.

Name of TV Show		
	😊	🙁
	😊	🙁
	😊	🙁
	😊	🙁
	😊	🙁

Appendix A: Reproducible Forms

The Kindness Coupon Book

Good for one bear hug

✂ Cut Out Coupon ✂

Good for a clean room

✂ Cut Out Coupon ✂

Good for one butterfly kiss or air kiss

✂ Cut Out Coupon ✂

Good for picking up toys

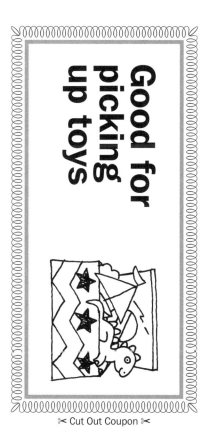

✂ Cut Out Coupon ✂

Good for 15 minutes of quiet play

✂ Cut Out Coupon ✂

Good for sharing

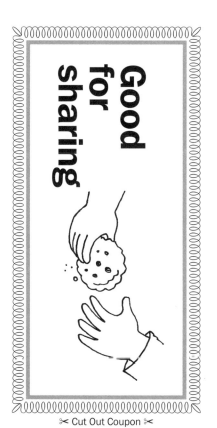

✂ Cut Out Coupon ✂

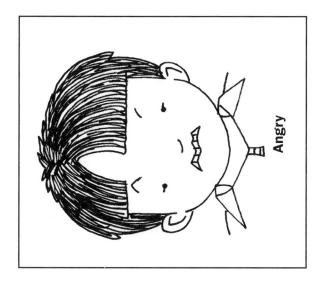

Angry

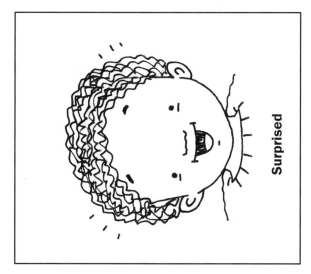

Surprised

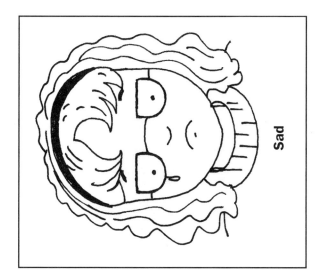

Sad

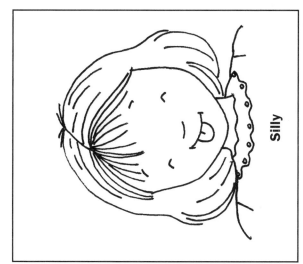

Silly

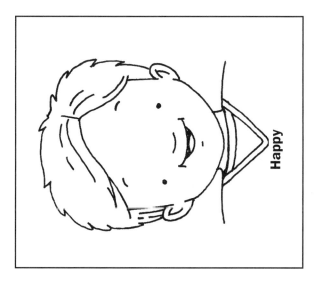

Happy

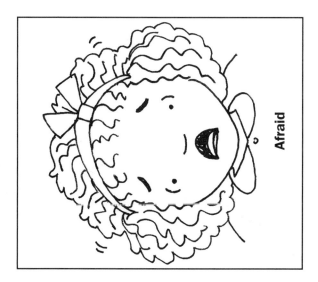

Afraid

My Day at School

Name: _____   Today's date: _____

I am trying to: _____
                                        Goal

The good news is: _____

🙂					

😢					

Comments: _____

_____

_____

Signature: _____
                                 Parent or Guardian

Helping Hands Pledge

I pledge to use my hands for helping.

_____

Child's name

take a time out

tear paper

cry awhile

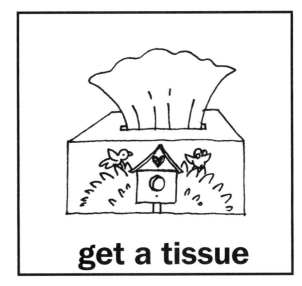

get a tissue

pound drums

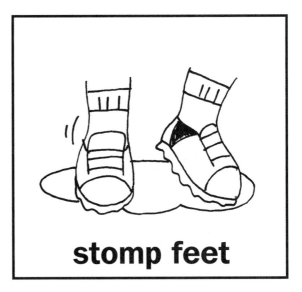

stomp feet

From *The Kindness Curriculum: Stop Bullying Before It Starts*, Second Edition, by Judith Anne Rice, © 2013.
Published by Redleaf Press, www.redleafpress.org. This page may be reproduced for individual or classroom use only.

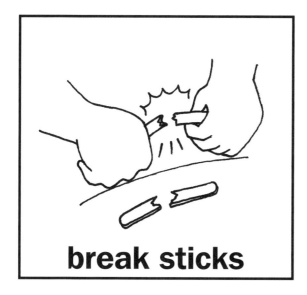

break sticks

roll around

jump

share

trade

take turns

flip a coin

talk about feelings

wait

stop and think

take a deep breath

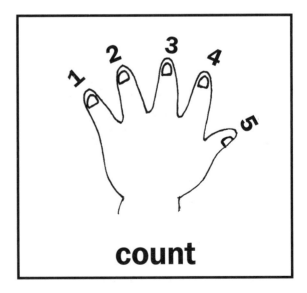

count

breathe with a tummy toy

blow bubbles

hug a stuffed toy

look at a book

sit and rock

stretch

Appendix B: Common American Sign Language Signs

Cleanup

Hungry

Come

Hurt

Happy

Line Up

Help

Listen

Mad

Sad

More

Scared

Please

Sick

Quiet/Calm/Peaceful

Silly

Sit

Thirsty

Stop

Tired

Thank You

Wait

Think

Walk

Recommended Resources

Children's Books

Agassi, Martine. *Hands Are Not for Hitting.* Minneapolis: Free Spirit, 2009.

Alborough, Jez. *Hug.* Cambridge, MA: Candlewick Press, 2000.

Asch, Frank. *Here Comes the Cat.* New York: Scholastic, 1989.

Avery, Charles E. *Everybody Has Feelings.* Lewisville, NC: Gryphon House, 1998.

Barton, Byron. *The Three Bears.* New York: HarperCollins, 1991.

Carle, Eric. *The Very Lonely Firefly.* New York: Philomel, 1995.

Catlow, Nikalas. *Oodles of Doodles.* Philadelphia: Running Press Kids, 2009.

Cook, Julia. *I Just Don't Like the Sound of No!* Boys Town, NE: Boys Town Press, 2011.

Crews, Donald. *Freight Train.* New York: Scholastic, 1978.

Dewdney, Anna. *Llama Llama Red Pajama.* New York: Scholastic, 2005.

Duksta, Laura. *I Love You More.* Naperville, IL: Sourcebooks Jabberwocky, 2007.

Dwight, Laura. *We Can Do It.* New York: Checker Board Press, 1992.

Eastman, P. D. *Sam and the Firefly.* New York: Random House, 1958.

Fine, Edith Hope. *Under the Lemon Moon.* New York: Lee & Low Books, 2002.

Garabedian, Helen. *Itsy Bitsy Yoga for Toddlers and Preschoolers: 8-Minute Routines to Help Your Child Grow Smarter, Be Happier, and Behave Better.* Cambridge, MA: Da Capo Press, 2008.

Gill, Bob. *The Present.* San Francisco: Chronicle Books, 2010.

Glass, Julie. *Counting Sheep.* New York: Scholastic, 2000.

Hanson, Warren. *Kiki's Hats.* Minneapolis: Tristan Publishing, 2010.

Henkes, Kevin. *Wemberly Worried.* New York: Scholastic, 2000.

Hughes, Shirley. *Giving.* London: Walker Books, 2005.

Kachenmeister, Cherryl. *On Monday When It Rained.* Boston: Houghton Mifflin, 1989.

Kaiser, Cecily. *If You're Angry and You Know It!* New York: Scholastic, 2004.

Katz, Karen. *Excuse Me! A Little Book of Manners.* New York: Grosset & Dunlap, 2002.

Kirk, David. *Little Miss Spider at Sunny Patch School.* New York: Scholastic, 2000.

———. *Miss Spider's Tea Party.* New York: Scholastic, 1994.

Lite, Lori. *Bubble Riding: A Relaxation Story.* Marietta, GA: Stress Free Kids, 2008.

Lovell, Patty. *Stand Tall, Mary Lou Melon.* New York: Scholastic, 2002.

MacLean, Kerry Lee. *Peaceful Piggy Meditation.* Park Ridge, IL: Albert Whitman Prairie Books, 2004.

Meiners, Cheri J. *Cool Down and Work Through Anger.* Minneapolis: Free Spirit, 2010.

———. *Respect and Take Care of Things.* Minneapolis: Free Spirit, 2004.

Muldrow, Diane. *The Happy Book*. New York: Scholastic, 1999.

Nelson, Michiyo. *My First 100 Words (Sign Language)*. New York: Scholastic, 2008.

Parker, David. *I Accept You as You Are!* New York: Scholastic, 2004.

———. *I Am Generous!* New York: Scholastic, 2004.

———. *I Am Responsible!* New York: Scholastic, 2004.

———. *I Can Make Good Choices!* New York: Scholastic, 2004.

———. *I Care about Others!* New York: Scholastic, 2004.

———. *I Show Respect!* New York: Scholastic, 2004.

Parr, Todd. *The Earth Book*. New York: Hachette, 2010.

———. *The Feel Good Book*. Boston: Little, Brown, 2002.

———. *The Feelings Book*. New York: Hachette, 2005.

———. *The I Love You Book*. New York: Hachette, 2009.

———. *The I'm Not Scared Book*. New York: Hachette, 2011.

———. *It's Okay to Be Different*. New York: Hachette, 2009.

———. *The Peace Book*. New York: Hachette, 2004.

Patricelli, Leslie. *Quiet Loud*. Somerville, MA: Candlewick Press, 2003.

Rice, Judith Anne. *Those Mean Nasty Dirty Downright Disgusting but . . . Invisible Germs*. St. Paul: Redleaf Press, 1989.

Richmond, Marianne. *If I Could Keep You Little . . .* Naperville, IL: Sourcebooks Jabberwocky, 2010.

Rotner, Shelley. *Feeling Thankful*. Minneapolis: Millbrook Press, 2000.

Scillian, Devin. *Memoirs of a Goldfish*. Chelsea, MI: Sleeping Bear Press, 2010.

Seeger, Laura Vaccaro. *Walter Was Worried*. New Milford, CT: Roaring Brook Press, 2005.

Selig, Josh. *Red and Yellow's Noisy Night*. New York: Sterling Children's Books, 2012.

Seuss, Dr. *Oh, the thinks You Can Think!* New York: Random House, 1975.

Shaw, Charles G. *It Looked Like Spilt Milk*. New York: HarperCollins, 1988.

Sierra, Judy. *Suppose You Meet a Dinosaur: A First Book of Manners*. New York: Knopf, 2012.

Silverstein, Shel. *The Giving Tree*. New York: Harper & Row, 1964.

Sister Susan. *Each Breath a Smile*. Berkeley, CA: Plum Blossom Books, 2001.

Slobodkina, Esphyr. *Caps for Sale: A Tale of a Peddler, Some Monkeys, and Their Monkey Business*. Boston: Addison-Wesley, 1968.

Swain, Gwenyth. *Smiling*. Minneapolis: Carolrhoda Books, 1999.

Thomas, Pat. *Stop Picking on Me*. New York: Barron's, 2000.

Tillman, Nancy. *On the Night You Were Born*. New York: Feiwel and Friends, 2005.

———. *Wherever You Are: My Love Will Find You*. New York: Feiwel and Friends, 2010.

Underwood, Deborah. *The Quiet Book*. Boston: Houghton Mifflin, 2010.

van Genechten, Guido. *Shhh . . .* Middleton, WI: Pleasant Company, 2001.

Verdick, Elizabeth. *Calm-Down Time*. Minneapolis: Free Spirit, 2010.

Waddell, Martin. *Owl Babies*. Somerville, MA: Candlewick Press, 1996.

Whitford, Rebecca. *Little Yoga: A Toddler's First Book of Yoga*. New York: Henry Holt, 2005.

Yolen, Jane. *How Do Dinosaurs Play with Their Friends?* New York: Blue Sky Press, 2006.

Books for Teachers

Coloroso, Barbara. *The Bully, the Bullied, and the Bystander.* New York: Harper Resource, 2003.

Crary, Elizabeth. *Without Spanking or Spoiling: A Practical Approach to Toddler and Preschool Guidance.* Seattle: Parenting Press, 1993.

Day, Jennifer. *Creative Visualization with Children: A Practical Guide.* Boston: Element Books, 2006.

Gillen, Lynea, and James Gillen. *Yoga Calm for Children: Educating Heart, Mind, and Body.* Portland: Three Pebble Press, 2007.

Houston, Jean. *The Possible Human: A Course in Enhancing Your Physical, Mental, and Creative Abilities.* Los Angeles: Tarcher, 1982.

Javna, John, Sophie Javna, and Jesse Javna. *50 Simple Things You Can Do to Save the Earth.* Rev. ed. New York: Hyperion, 2008.

Javna, Sophie. *The New 50 Simple Things Kids Can Do to Save the Earth.* Berkeley, CA: Andrews McMeel, 2009.

Lickona, Thomas. *Educating for Character: How Our Schools Can Teach Respect and Responsibility.* New York: Bantam Books, 1992.

Louv, Richard. *Last Child in the Woods: Saving Our Children from Nature-Deficit Disorder.* New York: Workman, 2008.

Petty, Jo. *Apples of Gold.* Norwalk, CT: C. R. Gibson, 1962.

Sarno, John E. *The Divided Mind: The Epidemic of Mindbody Disorders.* New York: Harper Perennial, 2006.

Smith, Charles A. *The Peaceful Classroom: 162 Easy Activities to Teach Preschoolers Compassion and Cooperation.* Beltsville, MD: Gryphon House, 1993.

Other Recommended Materials

www.bullylab.com. The Bully Lab is operated by Dr. Wendy Craig of Queen's University in Canada. The website offers research papers, strategies, and up-to-date information on efforts to stop bullying.

www.stopbullyingnow.com. Stop Bullying Now presents practical, research-based strategies for reducing bullying.

www.bullying.org. Bullying.org provides resources for the prevention and resolution of bullying, including support groups and several online courses.

www.stopbullying.gov. StopBullying.gov offers bullying prevention and response resources, as well as information regarding state-specific bullying policies and laws.

References

American Psychological Association, www. apa.org/about/policy/media.aspx

Cohen, Jennifer. 1994. "Hands-On Healing." *Elle*, February.

Evans, Betsy. 2012. "What Adults Can Do to Stop Hurtful Preschool Behavior before It Becomes a Pattern of Bullying." *Exchange* May/June: 56–59.

Field, Tiffany M. 2006. *Massage Therapy Research*. London: Churchhill Livingstone Elsevier.

Remig, Anita. 2009. *Childhood Developmental Disorders: Autism, Asperger's, Bipolar, ADHD, Nonverbal Learning Disability, Tourette's, and Other Related Disorders* (course workbook). Brentwood, TN: Cross Country Education.

Sarno, John E. 2006. *The Divided Mind: The Epidemic of Mindbody Disorders*. New York: ReganBooks.